What It Felt Like

From the Library Of

The Book Lady

Gail ♡

Read | Love | Learn

in memory of Mom

HENRY ALLEN

What It
Felt Like

LIVING IN THE AMERICAN CENTURY

PANTHEON BOOKS, NEW YORK

THEY UNDERSTOOD:

ERROLL MCDONALD, DEBORAH GROSVENOR,

STEPHEN REISS, AND DAVID VON DREHLE

All of the material in this book was originally published in
The Washington Post from September 20, 1999 to October 1, 1999

Illustration credits are on page 159.

Library of Congress Cataloging-in-Publication Data

Allen, Henry.
What it felt like/Henry Allen.
p. cm.
ISBN 0-375-42063-0
1. United States—Social life and customs—20th century. 2. United States—
History—20th century. I. Title.
E169 .A393 2000   973.9—dc21   00-024239

www.pantheonbooks.com

PRINTED IN THE UNITED STATES OF AMERICA
FIRST EDITION
2 4 6 8 9 7 5 3 1

For my children,

Hannah Rose, Peter Griffith,
and Nicholas Isaac De Wolf Allen,

and someday their children
and their children's children

CONTENTS

INTRODUCTION

You'd ask your mother, "What was it like in the olden days?"
Answer: Stricter, poorer, more polite.

No: You wanted to know what it felt like to be alive then.
How could she explain—the dusty heat of old television
sets, the smell of Vitalis on men's hair . . . women in gloves
that felt sexy touching your skin, the warmth . . . men who
whistled (with trills) and wore hats tipped to one side and
got killed in wars . . . the champagne disenchantment of the
tuxedo twenties, husbands who lost Depression jobs and hid
in their houses for shame, the October-morning energy of
the postwar forties, the barefoot LSD weddings when the
universe seemed a conspiracy in everyone's favor . . .

Charles Baudelaire, a hip nineteenth-century French poet,
said that each age has "a deportment, a glance, a smile of its
own."

In his high school yearbook, your father seems older at eighteen than you did at thirty-five. His age had a deportment of its own. So does yours.

Ages don't match decades, of course. Maybe the sixties ran from 1965 to 1975, but never mind. Some ages coincided with decades: the Roaring Twenties, the Depression thirties. Some didn't. Either way, decades are handy pigeonholes for lives and times.

No one denies the importance of history—newsreel dive bombers, Olympic medals, dates and facts. Yes, the *Titanic* sank, and Martin Luther King Jr. changed America.

But what did it feel like to be alive back then, when everything or nothing seemed possible? When you lay awake listening to train whistles that weren't so much noise as a heightening of your bedroom silence? When you smelled woodsmoke, walking home in the early dark?

What It Felt Like

Good Years

. . . a still brighter dawn of civilization . . .

What it felt like . . .

Back in the first decade of the twentieth century, the "Oughts," the Good Years, the Age of Confidence. People fought over solutions, not problems: the gold standard vs. free silver, the flying machine—tool or toy? And Teddy Roosevelt busted the trusts, started digging the Panama Canal, and sent the Great White Fleet around the world.

What it felt like just to walk down the street on a morning in early spring— The smell of dank, dark wool and the ragged sparking of streetcar wires, men with derbies and level stares, women holding skirts above the muck and manure, immigrants audacious with ambition, the dead, sweet smell of coal smoke, and soot on the last yellow, melting snow . . .

Back when health, wealth, and happiness seemed not just possible but inevitable, and there were Gibson girls with their confident, lifted hair and their hands in fur muffs . . . photographs of families lined up from tallest to shortest, like organ pipes . . . the whistle of stiff bristle brushes on porch floors . . . wiseacres saying, "Make like a hoop and roll out of here" . . . grimy children crippled in textile mills.

John D. Rockefeller said, "God gave me my money."

Things were dark and deliberate. Fathers knew best.

You want to know what it felt like to have the nervous system of a striker wrecking trains near Wilkes-Barre, Pennsylvania, or a baseball player sleeping in barns and living on bread and beefsteak, or a schoolteacher thinking about the science of Marie Curie and the bared legs of Isadora Duncan, then going home to hand her sealed pay envelope to Father.

In 1900, there were seventy-five million people in the forty-five states and by 1910 a million immigrants a year, and who knows what it felt like for each one of them?

Davy Jones, outfielder for the Chicago Cubs, would remember: "Back at the turn of the century, you know, we didn't have the mass communication and mass transportation that exist nowadays. We didn't have as much schooling, either. As a result, people were more unique then, more unusual, more different from each other. Now people are all more or less alike, company men, security-minded, conformity . . . that kind of stuff. In everything, not just baseball."

You already know Teddy Roosevelt shot bears and the Wright brothers flew an airplane on that cold beach in 1903. You've seen the crowd photographs. Everything seemed to happen in crowds: the masses huddled in slum flats, the sea-bathing ladies in bloomers, boys in knickers playing marbles. Things flashed around in newsreels: horses, smiles, top hats, parasols and dimity dresses.

Senator Albert Beveridge of Indiana announced, "God has marked the American people as his chosen nation to finally lead in the regeneration of the world. This is the divine mission of . . ."

Henry James said, "The will to grow was everywhere written large, and to grow at no matter what or whose expense." The expense of the working man? The immigrant? The farmer? Anarchists and atheists? The conquered Filipino?

But what it felt like is lost and gone forever, O my darling Clementine. No telling what it was like for W. K. Vanderbilt—the dining room of his Newport cottage had bronze furniture and Algerian marble walls—or for farmers driven off the land by railroads, or parents with children dying of diphtheria, whooping cough, typhoid, and malaria. Or for terrified families dressing up for the minister's visit. Or blacks: W. E. B. Du Bois, who went to Harvard and then studied racial theory in Germany, said American Negroes had a "two-ness . . . an American, a Negro, two souls, two thoughts, two unreconciled strivings."

But you have ideas. You have an idea of ashmen and icemen. The circus with miraculous foreigners in tights. Croquet. Resort hotels that burned down. So many blind people, harelips, clubfeet, hunchbacks. Chestnut trees. Hydrangeas. Vaudeville comics: "I sent my wife to the Thousand Islands for a vacation—a week on each island." Dogs: loyal Newfoundlands and smart pugs are good with children.

On Sunday evenings, Aunt Lil sings "'Tis the Last Rose of Summer." You cringe when the high note nears. Your mother mouths at you: "Don't." With the gramophone you can listen to Caruso singing "Vesti la giubba." He always makes the high note.

Machines will solve all our problems.

The *New York Times:* "We step upon the threshold of 1900 . . . facing a still brighter dawn of civilization."

The *Cheyenne Sun-Leader:* "Never has a year been ushered in with more promise."

Your father shaves with King Gillette's new safety razor. It's not as manly as the straight razor, somehow. But that Gillette! What a man! He says he's going to take the electricity from Niagara Falls and build a city for sixty million people! And he's not the only one—he's racing against Albert Love with his "Model City" and Love Canal.

Drain the swamps! Clear the forests! The city skyline gets higher every day, and the wind tears the smoke and steam out of stacks, banners of progress, an electric Camelot.

But how it felt . . .

You have an idea of dark houses with fringed couches and tables of golden oak.

A mother weeps in her bedroom for no reason she can tell. The doctor calls it neurasthenia. She feels asphyxiated, as if the whole world smelled like a clothes closet. She drinks another tablespoon of Lydia Pinkham's Vegetable Tonic, 18 percent alcohol.

Sitting by a kitchen window, a daughter wonders what real

love will be like and studies the Sears, Roebuck catalog ad for "La Dores Bust Food . . . for developing the bust and making it firm and round." There is linoleum on the floor. They can make anything now in factories. She watches the streetcar turn the corner with a waltzy pivot that isn't quite graceful, in the way that the metronome on the parlor organ isn't quite rhythmic. Aunt Lil says no machine will ever create beauty, though some European artists think art must be like machines in the future—anarchists, probably, or socialists. And what about the Pianola playing those beautiful rolls of sad Chopin! He lived with George Sand, a woman. Unmarried. And why not?

In his bedroom, a son lifts dumbbells and wonders if he is magnetic, masterful, and fascinating. Perhaps if he learned to play Ping Pong. Or smoked cigarettes. Or bought penny stocks . . . oil wells in Mexico . . . that turned him into the youngest millionaire in the history of Wall Street, and when he ran into old classmates they'd say, "If only we'd known then . . ."

Outside, an Italian family walks past with eyes you can't see into, the women shrouded in black, the men carrying knives, or so the son has heard. In the spring, they ask to pick your dandelions. For wine? Some people don't like Italians. They lynched eleven of them one day in New Orleans. But who was it who invented the radio? Marconi! Put that in your pipe and smoke it.

Off in the city, a father thinks about the lady "typewriters" clacking away outside his office in their shirtwaists with big shoulders that make their hands look small. He wears a high, stiff collar that makes his chin look bigger. Chins show character. He wishes his son cared more about character and less about what the young people call personality. Personality didn't dig the Panama Canal. It's one of those words that Walt Whitman slung around.

Wanting to have fame instead of a good reputation. Dancing the bunny hug. A fellow named Simon Nelson Patten saying that it is better to consume than to produce. Everything new and scientific. Magazines telling you the best ways to comb your hair and cook your dinner . . . Edward Bok and his *Ladies' Home Journal* calling for an end to corsetry. And *The Call of the Wild*, with Jack London telling you to live outdoors, free of the same civilization that publishes his books. Things feel a little unreal. Distant corporations can your food, light your house, ready-make your clothes without even measuring you, and give you music with machines when you used to make it yourself. *McCall's, McClure's,* all these magazines tell you how to beat rugs, cure female troubles, and raise your children. When Father was a boy, people knew these things. They didn't need some dude in a city to tell them. Still, we've got spine. After the San Francisco earthquake America turned down foreign offers of help and said we'd handle it ourselves, by God.

Father locks his desk. He wouldn't want anybody to open it and find Boccaccio's *Decameron,* which may be a classic in Europe but it's smut here in these United States.

On his way to the saloon, he dodges the clatter of a wagonload of shingles. He thinks of the fellow in the paper saying that soon the streets will be clean, silent, and uncrowded thanks to the automobile. It takes up less space than the horse and wagon and is quieter, with no iron-rimmed wheels or hooves on cobblestones with the sharp, dark crack that feels like it'll make your ears ring. But with fewer than 150 miles of paved roads in 1900, how soon can that happen?

Progress. Destiny. But will there be the men to make it happen? A doctor has written, "Is it not shameful to think of a big, well-built man, brought up on the farm . . . spending his days . . . whispering into a Dictaphone?" On the other hand, a commentator named John Bates Clark says, "A certain manly quality in our people gives assurance that we have the personal material out of which a millennium will grow."

Bill the bartender emerges from the haze of cigar smoke, pickle brine, and sawdust damp with beer. He says to Father, "Here's one you can tell the wife. It seems Paddy tells Mike that Mrs. O'Hara has died. 'Has she now, Paddy? And what did she die of?' 'Why, she died of a Tuesday.' "

"That's a corker," Father says, while he tries to figure it out. Ah: the way the Irish say "of" a Tuesday, not "on" a Tuesday. "A corker indeed, Bill."

We leave our family now, with Mother feeling better and going down the cellar stairs to fetch an apronful of potatoes sprouting the occasional white tendril, from a bin that smells mildewy and dusty at the same time. And apples for apple brown Betty. She sets the salt cod to soak.

The daughter decides on molded ice cream for her birthday party, angels for the girls and George Washingtons for the boys. In the spring, the milk tastes of the onion grass the cows have been eating. Will the ice cream taste of onions, too? Well, as long as Aunt Lil doesn't sing.

Someday this son and daughter will remember this house by the smell of hominy, pipe smoke, ill-fitted plumbing, rice pudding, cloves, radiator air, fried donuts, and the way you could follow summer into fall by the pies: strawberry, raspberry, blueberry and blackberry, apple, grape, pumpkin, yam. . . . Then it's winter, with canned peas, bread, and the root vegetables in the cellar bins: turnips, onions . . .

Outside, in the twilight chill, woodsmoke makes your nostrils flare. The sky over the city horizon twitches with glare from smelters. Down at the station, there's ice on the tracks. A locomotive, steam punching at the air, gets a little start and then the wheels lose purchase and they spin puffpuffpuff . . . puff, to silence, and it starts again.

The Idea
Is Change

. . . what youth always promises . . .

Years later, Virginia Woolf would write, "On or about December, 1910, human character changed. I am not saying that one went out, as one might into a garden, and there saw that a rose had flowered, or that a hen had laid an egg. The change was not sudden and definite like that."

Virginia Woolf was a little crazy, of course.

Then again, look at the photographs.

Before 1910—the Roosevelt years, the Age of Confidence—men with mustaches stare at the camera with the hard focus of self-command. Women look at it the way they'd look at an annoying policeman. Sometimes, lost in a focusless world of love or sublimity, they seem not to see it at all.

After 1910—the Belle Epoque and the Great War, an Age of Reform—men shave off their mustaches and try to capture the look of college boys, full of coy self-awareness and infinite possibility. Sometimes, with their cocked straw hats and their feet on the running board, they look a little weasely, like salesmen.

Women ignore their mothers' lessons on how a lady appears in public. They slowly jettison corsets, shed chaperones, and hike their hemlines over their ankles. They face the camera with an amused wiseguy wariness. Sometimes, for mischief, they pose with cigarettes. The face of sublimity starts to become the face of sexuality.

What you want is personality, not character. You want the frankness of Freud and the freedom of the Model T Ford. You want the nimbleness and passion of the movies, a mistake-free world where Douglas Fairbanks is always graceful and good and evil have given way to peril and desire, as in *The Perils of Pauline* and the seductions of Theda Bara, the original vamp.

The idea is to be up-to-date, to get aboard the Progress Train, to put an end to greed, ignorance, inequality, disease, addiction, autocracy, and the glooms of Victorian neurasthenia.

"I tried that alpine skiing and broke my leg."

"Say, Ted, we're in mixed company."

"Alice doesn't mind if I say 'leg' instead of 'limb,' Dexter."

"I think it's poor taste."

"Well, aren't you a sketch?"

A new look, a new ideal. You admire it in the face of Hobey Baker, hero of WASPdom and Princeton football and hockey, fighter pilot in World War I. Or John Reed, the Harvard revolutionary buried by the Kremlin Wall with Bolshevik heroes. Or even President Woodrow Wilson, former president of Princeton, smooth-faced and idealistic, a reformer.

He says, "I am a vague, conjectural personality, more made up of opinions and academic prepossessions than of human traits and red corpuscles." In short, he is not Teddy Roosevelt.

Pep. Adaptability. The gross national product triples in ten years. The national debt goes from $1 billion to $24 billion. Oh, boy. You just watch your Uncle Dudley, Mac, 'cause these United States are going to it. Child-labor laws. Pure-food laws. Free verse (Amy Lowell, Carl Sandburg) and free love (Isadora Duncan, Max Eastman). Prohibition of alcoholic beverages. Sending troops to put the Mexicans in their place. Doing the Daily Dozen exercises invented by Walter Camp, the Yale football coach. Suffragettes singing "Everybody's Doin' It Now" as they march up Fifth Avenue in their big 1912 hats and dresses.

"Doin' it, doin' it."

Youthfulness is a moral virtue. John Dewey, the progressive educator, attacks parents who "look with impatience upon immaturity, regarding it as something to be got over as rapidly as possible."

Max Eastman, the boy-faced editor, promises what youth always promises . . . that *The Masses* magazine will be "frank, arrogant, impertinent, searching for the true causes; a magazine directed against rigidity wherever it is found."

America is having one of its episodes of reforming its soul in the name of the American Dream . . . being very rich and very good at the same time. New soldiers of virtue called the Boy Scouts do a good deed every day. The educated classes listen to the renewal myths of Wagner. The whole country listens to a poem by Sarah Norcliffe Cleghorn:

The golf links lie so near the mill
That almost every day

The labouring children can look out
And watch the men at play.

College girls are the epitome of wholesomeness and progress. At the middlebrow cultural revivals called chautauquas, they tell stories to children, wear kilts, and perform with "Walter Eccles and the Four College Girls."

In the ocher air of a huge chautauqua tent, jawsmith Harry "Gatling Gun" Fogleman goes into his umpire's crouch and shouts at three hundred words a minute: "A negative thought is a poison as deadly as arsenic. Every morning now when I wake up I think positive thoughts and say, 'Fogleman, get out and get to it.' "

Dr. Russell H. Conwell bullies the lag-behinds: "I say you ought to be rich; you have no right to be poor."

Conwell and Fogleman sell themselves. They sell their audience on itself. The word *sell* has new meanings. It's not just about money and goods anymore; it's about personality and magnetism that can sell cars, birth control, educational toys, stock in land-scheme companies. Men who can sell are models for the masses with their appeals to pep, progress, and positive thinking. They are missionaries for the new religion of consumption, and for casting off the dark doughtiness of nineteenth-century production, all that old stuff about "a penny saved is a penny earned."

Henry Ford is a hero despite his assembly-line speedups and his anti-Semitism. He more than doubles pay to five dollars a day. He senses that higher wages will mean more buying. He has the same puzzled innocence that movie audiences will one day find in Gary Cooper, the youthful, roll-up-your-sleeves face of a man who lives only in the present. Ford says, "History is more or less bunk."

That's what the Great War will prove by demolishing the old order.

What a good idea demolishing the old order seems until it actually happens.

Until then, though, things are swell. You just play at demolishing the old order, never really suspecting you'll succeed. You dance the tango even—or especially—if the city fathers ban it. Ragtime is popular even though—or because—it comes from blacks.

> *Honey, honey, can't you hear*
> *funny, funny music, dear? . . .*
> *Everybody's doin' it, doin' it.*

You puzzle over Marcel Duchamp's painting, *Nude Descending a Staircase.*

"I saw where a fellow in the newspaper called it an explosion in a shingle factory."

"He's just jealous of a charming Frenchman. All you boys are."

"The Germans send us socialism, the Italians send us anarchism. The French send us this thing."

You sing Irving Berlin's "Alexander's Ragtime Band." You hunt, golf, and toboggan in a craze for outdoor sports. Your Protestant work ethic worries about this, but a magazine called *The Survey* reassures you, "Recreation changes leisure hours from liabilities to assets."

Ah, the metaphor of economics—who can gainsay the truths of the dismal science? Or any other science? Or progress? Or the Marxist forces of history? Or automobile companies instead of the village horse trader, or the federal government with its new income tax?

You get smaller in the swelling landscape of factories, dynamos, acts of Congress. You're part of a machine controlled by horns and whistles, bells summoning you in offices and at home, time-study experts watching you on the assembly line.

You feel like Nobody. You look for Somebodies to represent you in the legislature of the Republic of Modernity: movie stars, baseball players, radicals, Ziegfeld girls, Barrymores, union leaders, industrialists, Albert Einstein, inventors such as Thomas Edison and Harvey Firestone, authors such as Booth Tarkington, who writes about youth in his Penrod books.

You join the YMCA, or the swimming club where girls get to race in suits like the boys', or the crusade for Prohibition, or a group thrashing over the agnosticism of Robert Ingersoll. You stop saying grace at meals. You buy a car. You wire your house for electricity. There is so much energy in the air. Who can resist it?

The upper classes try. Yale and Princeton have built Gothic fortresses against modernity. They don't work, as F. Scott Fitzgerald, Princeton '17, will prove. The rich retreat to country seats in Far Hills, New Jersey, or Middleburg, Virginia. They don't work, either.

Fitzgerald, an Irish Catholic, would write of an upstart character viewing the uppers, "He knew the sort of men they were . . . the men who when he first went to college had entered from the great prep schools with graceful clothes and the deep tan of healthy summers. He had seen that, in one sense, he was better than these men. He was newer and stronger."

The rich used to be celebrities. Mrs. O.H.P. Belmont with her ineffable Chinese Ball at Newport! Now the diamond-decked dowagers are dreary. Immigrants take commerce and city governments away from them. The new rich buy their way into their Pullman cars and hotels.

The upper-class Senator Henry Cabot Lodge has warned for years that a million new immigrants a year will cause "a great and perilous change in the very fabric of our race."

Robert Bacon—Harvard athlete, partner of J. P. Morgan—will go off to war saying, "This world . . . our world . . . is not lucky enough to be snuffed out as was Pompeii. We have got to go through a long sickening decadence."

The war starts in Europe in August 1914.

We Americans are too busy with our reforms, we're too moral, we're "too proud to fight," as Wilson says. The *Wabash* [*Ind.*] *Plain Dealer* editorializes, "We never appreciated so keenly as now the foresight exercised by our fathers in emigrating to America." In 1915 people sing "I Didn't Raise My Boy to Be a Soldier."

In 1916, Wilson runs and wins with the slogan "He Kept Us Out of War." The war, though, is another huge, impersonal force, doin' it, doin' it. The Germans sink the *Lusitania*, killing 128 Americans. They send the Zimmerman telegram, offering to help Mexico reclaim lost territories in the United States.

Huns. Fritzies. Krauts.

On April 6, 1917, we declare. Everything changes. Americans can hardly wait for rationing, regimentation, censorship, the draft. Like working on Ford's assembly line or doing locomotive cheers for Yale, being at war makes us pieces of a machine. In boot camps, draftees march in uniform, having checked their individuality at the gate. Various days of the week are wheatless, meatless, gasless, and heatless. Women work in factories. Hemlines keep rising. Northern factory owners send out agents to hire southern blacks.

Wilson sells the war as the biggest reform movement of them all—the war to end all wars, to make the world safe for democracy. It's an easy sell. Is it ever.

Doin' it, doin' it.

George Creel, head of Wilson's Committee on Public Information, calls his job "a plain publicity proposition, a vast enterprise in salesmanship, the world's greatest adventure in advertising."

You stand at attention in restaurants whenever the band plays "The Star-Spangled Banner," which it does a lot, and there's a punch in the nose waiting for any man who doesn't. Sauerkraut becomes "liberty cabbage." German measles are "liberty measles." Boche books burn. A big movie is *The Kaiser, Beast of Berlin*. People see spies everywhere. Congress outlaws criticism of the government, the flag, the Red Cross, the YMCA, or any of our allies; fifteen hundred people are sentenced to jail. The Wobblies, a radical leftist union, are destroyed by a thousand arrests, setting up the Red Scare to come.

"Like most reformers, Wilson had a fierce and unlovely side," according to Charles W. Eliot, president of Harvard for forty years.

In nineteen months, America sends two million troops to Europe, after turning them into a fighting machine.

"Over There," as George M. Cohan sings, "Send the word, send the word over there / That the Yanks are coming."

The Yanks fight well. They are noted for their aggressiveness. About fifty-four thousand die in combat. More die of disease. The rest come back with memories of gas, barbed wire hung with corpses, a condition called "trench foot," typhoid, vermin (called cooties), and foreigners a lot of them don't particularly like. Froggies. Limeys. Krauts.

There are big parades but no statues, no generals running for president. In city squares, pigeons will continue to sit on statues of Grant, Lee, Sherman, and Jackson, not of Pershing. Wilson makes an idealistic fool of himself in treaty negotiations, the Bolshevik revolution rages in Russia, the Senate refuses to let America join the League of Nations. The war hasn't ended all wars, and the world isn't safe for democracy.

Everybody is sick of reform, idealism, promises, pep, and doin' it, doin' it. There are: disillusion, xenophobia, paranoia, persecution, propaganda, bomb throwing, strikes, lockouts. About 550,000 Americans die of the Spanish flu, and another twenty-five to forty million people around the world. Blacks who fought in France come home to race riots. Anarchists mail dynamite bombs to public men. The government rounds up radicals in the "Red Scare." Teddy Roosevelt—

frustrated, angry, grieving a son's death in the war—dies at sixty-one in 1919.

You are appalled when eight players for the Chicago White Sox are charged with conspiring to throw the World Series to the Cincinnati Reds. All are acquitted, but all are barred from baseball for life.

Outside the courtroom, a small boy confronts "Shoeless Joe" Jackson: "Say it ain't so, Joe."

This is what all the energy and reform come to. Virginia Woolf counsels that the newly changed human character must "tolerate the spasmodic, the obscure, the fragmentary, the failure." And: "We must reflect that where so much strength is spent on finding a way of telling the truth the truth itself is bound to reach us in rather an exhausted and chaotic condition."

1920–1930

Shocking, Therefore Modern

*. . . as if they needed
to be cured of something . . .*

Assume, for a moment, the existence of a beautiful young wife sitting alone under a Japanese lantern on a country-club porch.

Her name is Joan. She is a little tight. She has just decided not to launch a smoke ring of gratuitous contempt toward the next table, which has elected, at this late hour, to play mah-jongg.

Inside, an orchestra plays—the Clicquot Club Eskimos, the ones who play on the radio. They play "I Want to Be Loved by You," a song made unavoidable by Helen Kane, the Boop-Boop-A-Doop Girl.

Joan sings along, "Just you, and nobody else but you . . ."

"Pung!" says a woman named Violet at the mah-jongg table. "Or am I supposed to say 'Chow'?"

She turns and aims her cigarette holder at Joan.

"Where's the divine George?" she asks.

"Off in the men's grill, cornering the market in something," Joan says.

"I saw him talking oh-so-quietly on the phone."

"Don't be a cat, Violet. I've told him he can have all the girlfriends he wants, but he's so old-fashioned he doesn't want any."

I wanna be loved by you, just you . . .

We're all boop-boop-a-doop girls now, Joan thinks. Even the girls back home in Ohio. They learn their manners from radio, magazines, and movies: flapper slang like "scram" and "lounge lizard," so people will say, "She's got a good line." Cute pouts. Cocked heads. Slouched shoulders. The open-mouthed kiss as performed by Greta Garbo and John Gilbert. Shocking. Therefore modern. Or is it the other way around?

Modernity, in any case, seems to grant the right to invent yourself. Bob your hair, raise your hems, roll down your stockings, paint your lips, do the Charleston, and you're changed in a moment, the twinkling of a kohl-rimmed eye.

. . . you-oo-oo, boop-boop-a-doop.

Fireflies lilt over the eighteenth fairway. Joan remembers fireflies on nights when she and her mother knit sweaters for the boys fighting in France. What good did any of it do anyone—the war, the sweaters? Back then, the place to be was the Army, making the world safe for democracy. Now it's a country-club porch, drinking bootleg hooch, listening to jazz, and being disillusioned. Who wouldn't be after the chaos in Europe and the strikes and bombs and Red Scare here, and the horrible Ku Klux Klan with its parades and lynchings? And the hypocrisy of Prohibition: Al Capone, with his army of bootleggers, is a bigger hero than the president. People get their souls saved by preachers you see in the tabloids, an ex-baseball player named Billy Sunday and Aimee Semple McPherson, who pulled that stunt about being kidnapped.

An Eskimo sings through a megaphone: "In the morning, in the evening, ain't we got fun?" A chorus of banjos answers yes, O yes.

Having fun might not seem such a duty back in Ohio, Joan thinks. Do people still have fun in Ohio? The farmers get poorer, the preachers rail about Darwin and evolution, and the Rotary Club is full of men going prematurely everything—bald, fat, sexless, smug. They build Kozy Kabin Motor Kourts. They recite lines from Bruce Barton's book

The Man Nobody Knows, about how Jesus was the "founder of modern business" because he understood the concept of service.

If only Jesus could service their Buick so it started in the rain. If only George would buy her a Jordan roadster so she could be the girl in the advertisement, racing against a cowboy who whips his horse with his hat.

"Somewhere west of Laramie," the ad says, there's a car that's "built for the lass whose face is brown with the sun when the day is done of revel and romp and race. She loves the cross of the wild and the tame. . . ." Yes: a car that would make her feel reinvented every time she got into it.

But no. George drives a Buick. Puts every cent into the market. He's working on his second million.

He gets reinvented by reading the stock tables at breakfast. He's a self-made man. His life is an endless self-improvement course. He gargles Listerine to prevent halitosis. He studies books like *Masterful Personality* by Orison Swett Marden. He recites the words of Émil Coué: "Day by day, in every way, I am getting better and better." Strange how people now act as if they all need to be cured of something. Sexual repression. Boredom. Idealism. Cynicism.

The Eskimos play the Charleston. Naked shoulders, pigeon toes, and knock knees flail away in dresses that hang from the shoulders instead of rising from the waist like the dresses her mother still wears. Her mother taught her that beauty was grace and presence. Now it's drape and cuteness.

Men are cute, too. They have shiny hair and they chop away at the floor with their shiny shoes. Like machines. They wear tuxedos. All men do now, even gangsters at those incredible funerals with tons of flowers.

Joan watches George stride across the ballroom in his tuxedo. Who was he talking to on the phone?

He shoots his jaw and looks manly, as if he were posing for an Arrow Collars ad. Not manly like Teddy Roosevelt, with big belly and bluffness, but manly like fighter pilots in the Great War, all angular youth. Mayor Jimmy Walker with New York showgirls on his arm. Ernest Hemingway sitting in a Paris café being ironic.

"A bunch of journalists and critics and that crowd have crashed the party," George announces.

"Sit down, darling, before everybody starts listening to you. What crowd?"

"Oh, those people who write about how this country is

savage and ignorant and then they put up sculptures that look like airplane propellors."

"Ssshh," she says. "They're sitting two tables down, saying how there are no more morals because Einstein proved everything was relative."

"I'm not talking about Einstein," George says.

"Is that H. L. Mencken with the cigar? He just said something about the 'drivel of idealism.' "

"You're not listening to me."

"I'm a little tight," says Joan. "Your bootlegger forgot to water the scotch."

"There was this couple out there in a Pierce Arrow," George says. "In the back seat. Right there in the Piping Hills Country Club driveway. Like animals."

"That's what you don't understand," says Joan. "We aren't *like* animals, we *are* animals."

"That's that Freud bunk again," George says. "And the anthropologists, too—Margaret Mead talking about free love in Samoa."

"Margaret Mead doesn't say we're animals," she says. Oh, nuts to George. He won't answer anyway. He's being patient but firm, the way his father taught him to be with women, back when women didn't drive Jordan roadsters and get tight. My, she's tight.

"I'm feeling a bit ossified," Joan says. "I need to move around."

With the airy precision of a woman determined not to stumble in her high heels, she ambles to the porch rail where the beautiful firefly darkness begins.

"Are you all right?"

" 'My candle burns at both ends; it will not last the night,' " she says cheerfully. "Edna St. Vincent Millay wrote that. She went to Vassar, like me. You know what they say about Vassar girls."

"Not my Vassar girl."

"I see a crusade for us, George," Joan says. "Yes, let's go be missionaries to flappers and flaming youth. Maybe we can save them from the Algonquin Round Table and Louis Armstrong and flagpole sitters and intellectuals making fun of the booboisie, and, well, everything."

Joan sees that George is afraid she's about to make a scene. Well, why not make one, then?

"Who were you talking to on the telephone?" she pleads. "Please, George, tell me it was your girlfriend, a chorus girl named Vilma in a cold-water flat in Greenwich Village, and she's threatening to send your letters to the tabloids."

"It was that damn bootlegger," George says, patient but firm. "He wants me to settle up. Thinks the market is going to crash."

"It isn't, though," Joan says. "Everybody says it isn't."

"Except my bootlegger," George says.

Oh, well. What a beautiful night. Fireflies. The smell of cut grass. The smell of money. What more could you ask? But it's all so sad, somehow. Like F. Scott Fitzgerald saying, "All Gods dead, all wars fought, all faiths in man shaken."

She blows a smoke ring into the darkness. She notices that the journalists don't quite listen to one another; they're all too busy concocting their next quip. Is that Harold Ross, the editor who said the *New Yorker* wouldn't be edited for the "little old lady from Dubuque"?

Joan watches a man raise large, confident lids over large, confident eyes. Walter Lippmann? With the authority of a man who seems to speak directly from his forehead, Lippmann offers an opinion: "What most distinguishes the generation who have approached maturity since the debacle of idealism at the end of the war is not their rebellion against the religion and the moral code of their parents, but their disillusionment with their own rebellion."

"Boop-boop-a-doop," Joan says, with the startling loudness of a hiccup. Lippmann looks at her and leans back in his chair.

Leaning is the correct posture now. Flappers in unbuckled galoshes leaning against roadsters, Will Rogers standing on stage in that cowboy slouch with all his weight on one hip. As if people had listened to so much jazz they'd become personally syncopated. She thought about an Edward Steichen picture of Rudolph Valentino leaning about seventeen degrees off vertical, with one hand in a pocket and the other holding a cigarette. Yes. Somehow leaning explained everything.

Better tell the journalists about it. Her duty, really. Like telling firemen about a fire.

"I've figured it out," she says. "You should write about it, you people. Here it is: This is an era in history when everybody seems to be leaning."

Eyebrows rise. Jaws drop.

"Leaning," she says. "Like the Prince of Wales with his navy hat cocked over one eye, or all of you slouched down in your chairs. You can't imagine Teddy Roosevelt leaning. . . ."

"She's right!" someone shouts.

"No," someone else says. "This is the era of flatness. All these women in dresses that look better on hangers. Flat chests. Flat hips. Everybody looking down at the earth from airplanes and seeing that it's flat, flat, flat. Paintings as flat as the hieroglyphics on King Tut's tomb."

"Teddy Roosevelt was round," Joan says. "Fred Astaire is flat. Flat as a paper doll."

She feels hands on her elbows.

"Joan," says George.

She turns and kisses his cheek for the benefit of the journalists. "Am I making a fool of myself?"

"I'll tell you what everything is," George says. "I know I'm the capitalist sort you fellows make fun of, but everything wrong with this country is summed up in two words: flagpole sitters."

"Oh, darling, how wonderful," Joan says. "You're tight, too."

"I'm serious. Shipwreck Kelly sits on top of a pole for a few weeks doing nothing but sitting there, and now he's famous. He's just famous for being there, is all. Like Texas

Guinan gets famous for running speakeasies and saying 'Hello, sucker.' Or these athletes—the last time I heard, baseball was a team sport, but now all you hear about is Babe Ruth. Charles Lindbergh is a god now. For what? People have been flying across the Atlantic for years. But New York drops a ton of of ticker tape and torn-up phone books on him because he did it alone and he's so damned good-looking. He just took his flagpole from New York to Paris."

"You can't make fun of Lindbergh," someone says. "I think there's a law against it."

"How about Coolidge?" someone snaps at George. "There's a flagpole sitter for you. Saying, 'The business of America is business.' That's like saying the president of the United States is president."

They're starting to make fun of him, Joan thinks. She wants to protect him; there's something doomed and noble about his Republican earnestness. She considers blowing a smoke ring at the journalists but a breeze has come up. A cool breeze, just cool enough to make everyone on the porch seem stranded.

"I'm chilly," Joan says. "Do you know where I left my wrap?"

They escape. As they walk down the drive to their Buick,

the club drifts away behind them like a cruise ship. The lovers' Pierce Arrow has a flat tire, she notices. The lovers are gone.

"What would it mean if the stock market crashed and didn't come back?" Joan asked. "We'd have to live in a little house with only one servant, and you'd have to get a job where you had to do something real—invent fire hydrants or something. We complain now that we're bored, but we'd be terribly nostalgic for these times, wouldn't we? We'd teach our children to be nostalgic, too. And they'd teach their children. America will be nostalgic for these days until the year 2000. Except it will be like a lost chord—nobody will be able to figure out how we made meaninglessness seem so meaningful. And the thing is, if you can figure that out, what else do you need?"

"A good market," George says. "Just till the end of the year. I'm getting out in 1930. I promise."

"Will you buy me a Jordan roadster then and make love to me in it? Right here at the Piping Hills Country Club? Just me and nobody else but me?"

With the immense delight of a dull man getting off a good line, George puts his arm around Joan and says, "Boop-boop-a-doop."

What Isn't There

. . . damned if you do,
damned if you don't . . .

It's not like you go out on your porch and see the Depression standing there like King Kong.

Most neighborhoods, things look pretty normal, not that different than before the Crash. Paint peels on houses. Cars get old, break down. Nothing you'd notice right away. Kids play with their Buck Rogers ray guns. You go to the movies on dish night; you like the Fiesta Ware, very modernistic, red and blue.

Definitely, you read in the papers how in Chicago unemployment hit 50 percent, and men were fighting over a barrel of garbage; or in the Dust Bowl, farmers saying they'll lynch judges who foreclose on their property. That kind of thing. It's terrible.

But most places you don't see it. Roosevelt can say, "I see one-third of a nation ill-housed, ill-clad, ill-nourished." That leaves two-thirds where you don't see the hobo jungles, people lined up for government cheese. You feel what isn't there: it's like on Sunday afternoon, the quiet. You don't hear carpenters driving nails, you don't hear rivet hammers going in the city.

Fewer cars in town, just the stoplights rocking in the wind. You don't hear as many whistles: factory, railroad. You don't hear as many babies crying. People are afraid to have them. Down the block there's a man you don't see outside his house on workdays. He doesn't want the neighbors to know he's out of work again. Smoking cigarettes, looking out the window, waiting for *Amos 'n' Andy* to come on the radio.

He was a sales manager for a train-wheel company, back when the railroads were buying thirteen hundred locomotives a year. In 1932, they don't buy any. The company lets him go. He takes a job selling insurance. Insurance companies know you can sell policies to your family, your friends. When you can't sell any more, they let you go.

He sells vacuums, then encyclopedias, door to door. He ends up spending all day at the movies. He won't let his wife apply for relief. He's too proud. His son quits high school— he's out west to build a national park for the Civilian Conservation Corps, at thirty dollars a month. He sends most of it home so his mother can get her teeth fixed. And put dimes in the chain letters she mails out.

People write songs about tramps—"Brother, Can You Spare a Dime"—but you don't see them unless they come to your back door; people say they make a chalk mark on your fence if you're good for a handout. You've never found any mark, but they keep coming. You wonder how they survive.

One guy's feet are coming out of his shoes, but he's got a new tweed overcoat.

You say, "Glad to see you got a warm coat."

He says, "I got it raking leaves for an undertaker. They're good for clothes."

You see the Depression in the papers, in the magazines and newsreels: heads getting busted during strikes, dust storms burying cows, Reds parading through Wall Street with their fists in the air, shouting, "Bread, bread," or Huey Long, the Louisiana Kingfish himself, flapping his arms and shouting about "every man a king," Roosevelt looking over plans for electric power dams in the Tennessee Valley, his cigarette holder pointing up—the columnists say "at a jaunty angle." And the lines: in front of soup kitchens, relief offices, banks that are failing. And cute stuff: kids hang a sign that says "Depression" on a snowman and throw snowballs at it.

Then you're looking at blood and bullet holes from gangster shoot-outs, a girl drinking a glass of beer at the end of Prohibition, kids jitterbugging to Benny Goodman or Count Basie. Bathing beauties, bathing beauties, bathing beauties, and the glamour girls of café society . . . Brenda Diana Duff Frazier, the debutante of the year, smiling from her table at El Morocco or the Rainbow Room. No Depression there.

The Yankees win the pennant. Jesse Owens makes the Olympic team. Soldiers goose-step in front of Hitler or Mussolini or Stalin. Hemingway in the Spanish Civil War, glamorous in that manly way that took over from everybody wanting to look like boys in the 1920s, including the women.

The new styles: women have waists and busts again. They aren't supposed to look bored anymore, either. You don't get a job, relief, whatever, looking bored. Hemlines go back down. People say hemlines go up and down with the stock market, but that's hooey. The idea is to look more mature. Women's hats, though—feathers, veils, flowers. You read how a woman in a New York tearoom put a bread basket on her head and nobody knew the difference.

From the Crash till Roosevelt's first term, in 1933, everybody tried to keep living the way they had. It didn't work. Things had to change. Now *Fortune* magazine says the Flaming Youth of the 1920s is gone and we've got a "generation that will not stick its neck out. It keeps its shirt on, its pants buttoned, its chin up, and its mouth shut."

If you're older, during all those good years you felt like a self-made man, so now when you're cleaning out your desk, boarding up your store, you feel like a self-ruined man.

The preachers and businessmen all have something to blame: moral breakdown, a natural cycle, the Wall Street short sellers, the installment plan, high tariffs, low tariffs, the British, the Russians. That didn't use to be the American way, to blame anybody but yourself. Lot of things have changed.

Your father's job was to build towns, raise wheat. Your job is to buy things. A poster shows a guy with a lunch bucket and a paycheck; his wife smiling at him. The words say, "When you BUY an AUTOMOBILE You GIVE 3 MONTHS WORK to Someone Which Allows Him to BUY OTHER PRODUCTS."

If you ain't got the mazuma to spend, you don't count.

You hear a husband and wife arguing.

"Why don't you fix cars?" the wife asks. "Every time I go downtown I see a new garage. Everybody's car is breaking down."

"I'm not a car mechanic. I'm a machinist," the husband says.

"It's money," she says.

"You're right, that's the sad part," he says. "Back when we got married, I had a trade. I'm a machinist. Then they bring in the efficiency experts with their clipboards, timing every move I make. They turn me from a machinist into a machine. I say, what the hell, it's still good money. Then they take away the money. What a mug I was to think we were on Easy Street. What have I got left?"

"You've got a wife and kids wearing cardboard in the bottom of their shoes," she says.

"Take in a show," he says.

People think you get away from the Depression at the movies, but the Hollywood types know there're hard times and unrest everywhere, and they don't just show them in the newsreels.

When Mickey Mouse first came along in *Steamboat Willie*, he was a mean little pest, but now Walt Disney is making him the common man, a hero like the common man in the murals government artists paint in post offices. The little guy as hero. That's a change, all right.

In the Thin Man movies, they make William Powell the pal of every working stiff in the city: he stops to gas with the iceman, the new butcher, the local pickpocket before he goes off to drink martinis someplace with white telephones and Myrna Loy sliding around in a bathrobe you could wear for a coronation. Witty as hell. You walk out of the theater wanting to not give a damn like that.

She says, "I read you were shot five times in the tabloids."

He says, "It's not true. He didn't come near my tabloids."

Here's the power of the movies: you read that John Dillinger and his gang pretend to be a movie company on location in front of a bank in Sioux Falls, South Dakota. The whole city gawks while inside, the pretend actors clean out the bank.

The FBI guns Dillinger down outside a movie theater in Chicago. You hear the coroner sent part of his anatomy to the Smithsonian Institution in Washington, it was that big.

You hear a lot of stories.

You hear about a smart guy, out of work. He starts an

employment agency and takes the first job he was supposed to fill.

The stories about stockbrokers jumping out windows on Black Tuesday, October 29, 1929. The suicide rate was higher right before the Crash than after it, but nobody wants to hear that.

Everybody's brother-in-law knows a banker who works as a caddy now at his old country club.

In 1931, Cameroon, in West Africa, sends New York City a check for $3.77 to help the starving. Immigrants are going back to Europe by the shipload. Makes you feel bad.

When Roosevelt closes all the banks in 1933, you hear about one lucky woman who overdrew her account the day before.

In Deming, New Mexico, the Southern Pacific yard dicks drive so many hobos off the trains, the town has to hire a constable to drive them back on.

On the Grand Concourse in the Bronx they have a poorhouse for the rich—the Andrew Freedman Home, a mansion—so when the rich lose their money they don't have to live like the poor.

Eleanor Roosevelt is out visiting the poor and she sees a

boy hiding a pet rabbit. His sister says, "He thinks we are not going to eat it. But we are."

Babies go hungry while farmers in Iowa dump their milk trying to get the price up to where they can keep producing milk so babies won't go hungry.

Herbert Hoover himself believes that "many persons left their jobs for the more profitable one of selling apples."

The apple story is enough to make you think the Reds are right.

In 1930, right after the Crash, Washington State has a bumper crop of apples. Too many to sell. So instead of dumping them, they give them to vendors on credit. Next thing, men are lined up in Wall Street, wearing homburg hats and selling apples, five cents apiece. There are so many of them they start cutting prices on each other. At the same time, the apple growers get greedy: they raise the prices and don't cull the rotten ones. Pretty soon you can't make any money in the apple business, and it's all over.

The feeling is, damned if you do, damned if you don't. Like playing the Irish Sweepstakes. A lot of gambling now: bingo, punch boards, slot machines, the numbers.

Some people say communism will save us. Guys in black

hats and leather jackets at the union meetings. They know how to organize, they know what they think, but you wonder if they could sell apples any better than anybody else. People are scared of the Reds. A witness tells the House Un-American Activities Committee that out in Hollywood, Shirley Temple is a "stooge of the Reds" for sending money to the Spanish Loyalists. A little girl!

They say J. Edgar Hoover and the FBI will save us from the Reds, the Nazi spies, the gangsters. The kids love him, running around in their Junior G-Man badges.

They say Roosevelt will save us. He comes on the radio in his fireside chats, but not like Father Coughlin yelling about Reds and Jews; just talking. "My friends," he says. Like he knows you know he knows how you feel. He doesn't have it all figured out like the Reds or Huey Long. He'll try anything until the Supreme Court knocks it down. The problem is, things don't get much better. He says in 1932, "The only thing we have to fear is fear itself." Years go by and he's still right.

And science will save us. You go to the World's Fairs in Chicago and New York and learn how technocrats will build things out of plastic and beryllium bronze—the World of Tomorrow. No class struggle because science will have solved all the problems. You'll never have to sweat out a toothache or watch your boss's face to see if he's going to replace you with his son-in-law. All you need is brains, not courage. You wonder, though, Is that the American way?

What you know for sure is that whoever's running things right now, it isn't you.

First it was the trusts and the railroads that took control of your life, then Wall Street and advertising, and now it's Roosevelt's Brain Trust and the alphabet agencies: NRA, PWA, WPA, CCC, CWA. They prove everything with numbers and polls: 37 percent of housewives spend 22 percent more hours blah blah . . .

Everything's scientific. You don't just get married, you go to college and take a course in "modern marriage." Half the babies in the country are born in hospitals. A mother isn't supposed to feed her baby with her own milk. It doesn't have enough of the vitamins they've discovered now. Science turns into a fashion. White tile and stainless steel, waitresses wearing white uniforms. Progress.

One day the out-of-work salesman and his wife down the block are gone. Not a word of good-bye.

The machinist gets a job in an airplane factory, making bombers.

When your nephew comes to the breakfast table, he swings his leg over the back of the chair, like Clark Gable in *It Happened One Night*. Or Mickey Rooney in the Andy Hardy movies with Judy Garland.

Men don't wear tops on their bathing suits anymore.

Girls wear saddle shoes and apron dresses. They drink Cokes in drugstores. The soda jerk thinks they all have a crush on him, his white paper hat cocked to one side.

If you want to show your social consciousness, you don't have a "cleaning woman" anymore, you have a "cleaning lady."

How is vaudeville going to stand up to movies and radio? What will Milton Berle do for a living?

Modern furniture gets crazier. You see a picture of a bedroom in Hollywood with these reading chairs only Ming the Merciless could be comfortable in, and a laminated wood bed you could put on a Mayan funeral barge, everything tapered—table legs, lamps, vases.

You hear stories that Roosevelt, the British, and the Jews are trying to get us into a war.

Huey Long gets shot dead in Baton Rouge.

And there's the feeling you hardly notice after a while—a shabby feeling, dust and phone wires, a cold spring wind, things exposed, like on Sunday afternoon, the quiet.

The Energy
of Fate

. . . anything is possible . . .

Pack of Pall Malls in my pocket, Vitalis on my hair, penny loafers, sport coat with the shirt collar spread over it so I'm all shoulders and shoes walking into the drugstore. Whistling "Fools Rush In" with all the trills.

And I know every jitterbug break in the book.

My girlfriend, Arlene—sharp little bobbysox, sweater and pearls—says when popular dances get violent it means there's going to be a war.

I say, "Arlene, I don't think you're gonna start any wars."

She takes it all wrong, like it's an insult. Dames, who can figure them? She won't let me past first base, anyway.

Some things are more important than women. Bogart knows that: check out *The Maltese Falcon* and *Casablanca*.

DiMaggio hits safe in fifty-six straight games. You can get work. I got a job in the new government plant. Women working there now, even some colored guys.

Building stabilizer fins for the British on Lend-Lease.

Build them for the Eskimos for all I care, as long as we stay out of the war.

My old man was in the last war, and he's still sorry. He says, "Make the world safe for democracy. You bet, pal."

The Germans and the Japanese are nuts, that newsreel of Hitler dancing around when the French surrendered. Let them fight it out over there.

Then it's a Sunday morning. I'm out back trying to get my jalopy to start, and Mom hollers out the back door with this amazed, right-now sound in her voice. I run inside. She's not just listening to the radio, it's like she's watching it. I hear "Japanese" and "Pearl Harbor." Goddamn sneak attack.

The next morning, there's a line around the block at the recruiting station. I'm in it. Forget my old man, forget the America Firsters and the isolationists, forget my job—let Arlene do it.

Everybody agrees. That's what's so wild. Businessmen, professors, Republicans, Democrats, the unions, Wall Street, everybody. Has this ever happened before in this country? It's like what they say now: Forget it, Mac—there's a war on. Even the ads:

Cordley Electric drinking fountains have gone to sea!
Mogul Metallizing Gives Wings to Paratroopers!
Joe's the boy for WORK. And till we measure the Axis part-
ners for some snug wood vests, he'll have little time for play. So
Joe keeps his morale hitched high with long-wearing clothes . . .
    Scratch One Zero! Wherever Navy buzzard-busters swing into
action, you'll probably find Synthane!

Bleak horizontal war world: boot-camp drill fields in
predawn . . . drill sergeant's power-grinder voice YOUR
OTHER LEFT JACKSON YOU GODDAMN HILL-
BILLY . . . the heft of new web belts and canvas packs, the
weight of a helmet YOU WILL KEEP THAT CHIN
STRAP BUCKLED YOU ARE NOT SOME MOVIE
ACTOR . . . the hikes—CLOSE IT UP BACK THERE
YOU'RE LAGGING—with fifty pounds of pack, entrench-
ing tool, canteen, extra boots, gas mask, M1 rifle . . . staring
at the back of somebody's neck, everything in rows . . .
bunks, barracks, the latrine with its rows of commodes whose
seats are always warm from the last guy . . . the loneliness. . . .

Please don't call long-distance this Christmas . . . war calls
come first.

Vitality Shoes Fit the Victory Tempo!

What Comfort and Efficiency with Tampax . . . Women's monthly sanitary problems are more acute during wartime.

You're writing a soldier in Italy. You know he isn't in love with you, he's in love with the idea of having a girl back home, the way you were in love with having a soldier thinking about you over there. It feels wrong to write him a Dear John letter, and it feels wrong not to. Did you lead him on? Then he gets killed and you cry and cry without being sure what you're crying for.

Sometimes you wish you were married. *Dearest Jim, You are the proud papa of a six-pound, three-ounce bouncing baby boy. . . .* But a girl down the street was just home from the maternity ward and the staff car pulls up, the officer knocks on the door to tell her that her husband was killed at Guadalcanal.

You keep hearing about them. Johnny Vudraskis, the butcher's son, got a posthumous Medal of Honor in North Africa. Your second cousin Bill missing at sea . . . you had the worst crush on him in Atlantic City that time.

Dance with sailors at the canteen, put their hats on your head and look cute, hair bouncing.

Your best friend has a little girl. They go to the beach, and the little girl keeps running up to boys in uniform and saying, "Are you my daddy?"

Get a job at an ammo plant. Have to work with a chemical called tetryl, it dyes your hair orange. You don't want other women thinking you dye your hair. You get another job typing at the Office of Price Administration. People complain about their rations. Rich woman in a huff: she has a six-bedroom house, you give her fuel oil for two? Shortages of meat, gas, stockings . . . some women color their legs brown like stockings and draw the seam lines up their calves with a mascara pencil.

Government poster says:

> *Use it up,*
> *Wear it out,*
> *Make it do,*
> *Or do without.*

Warm thick smell of berthing compartments on troopships, like fresh bread made out of old undershirts and cigarette butts. Stack the troops four high on canvas pallets . . . hear water rushing past the hull . . . rough weather . . . guy on top rack upchucks, it drips . . . guys skidding and falling in it . . . all these bodies and you're lonely, bored, scared . . . crap games, decks of cards so worn they're soft . . . skipper says all the Betty Grable and Rita Hayworth cheesecake has to come down.

After 1942 and the battles of Midway and the Coral Sea, you know we're going to win, it's just a job now . . . North Africa, moving up Italy . . . you hear about the zoot-suit riots in Los Angeles, GIs beating up Mexicans . . . same stuff in World War I, race riots, people go crazy during wars . . . you're writing to a girl, she sends you her picture but then she stops writing. . . .

Then a strip of land like a pencil mark on the wall. Landing craft circle for hours, and you're scared, praying to Saint Mike, the embattled sword guy . . . rows of bullets flash in the water, then the artillery zeroes in . . . explosions that move the whole world sideways, hammer you down into yourself, and then one so close it feels like it blows the soul right out of you . . . the amazements of blood, the back-of-the-throat smell of bodies in the sun . . . the terrible truth of the first dead enemy you see—he's just a guy like you . . . rubble, whores . . . Roosevelt dies, a nation mourns, you're walking through mud, looking for a C-ration with fruit cocktail.

> *Life's reet when you dig that beat,*
> *on the sunny, sunny side of the street!*
> —Tommy Dorsey and the Clark Sisters
> (the Sentimental Sisters of Swing).

In *House Beautiful,* Corporal Donald K. Peterson writes about his dream house: "There will be a new and changed United States, and I want my house to be in keeping with this new spirit . . . a home in which the use of transparent plastic and the frosty silver of duraluminum will fit."

We drop atom bombs on Hiroshima and Nagasaki. *Time* magazine tells us, "The knowledge of victory was as charged with sorrow and doubt as with joy and gratitude" because the bomb created a "bottomless wound in the living conscience of the race."

Unless you're on Okinawa, staging to invade the home islands of Japan.

Bright wild air of back-home America: traffic jams, factory whistles, and the colors—wallpaper, curtains, magazine stands, Texaco signs—the smell of sunlit car upholstery, your girlfriend's hair . . . the future sparkles in front of you like a weekend ocean. Everything is possible.

Vets hang around the soda shop. They're in the 52-20 Club—the government gives them twenty dollars a week for a year. They wear their old high school clothes, but they haven't lost their combat faces yet, a hard, too-calm look. Sitting in the booths all day.

"Going to be another depression, you always get them after wars. Then you end up fighting another war."

"Next war, pal, nobody has to go because it'll be all atom bombs and V-2 rockets, and there won't be nobody left."

"Next thing you hear about atomic power it'll be under the hood of your car and heating your house."

"Russians won't have the atom bomb for ten years."

"House, that's a laugh. GI Bill gives you a two-thousand-dollar secured loan, and try and find one."

"All I want is a car, but I'm not bribing some salesman to get it."

"They'll put up prefab houses with radiant heating and electric kitchens."

"Sure, when the construction unions stop shutting down the prefab plants, then you'll get prefabs."

"Unions are full of Communists. Truman ought to get after them."

"You seen lady wrestling yet?"

Like the song says (girls in saddle shoes, walking down the street, snapping fingers and singing together):

> *You've got to ac-cent-tchuate the positive,*
> *E-lim-in-ate the negative . . .*

Quonset huts go up on the university golf course for veterans. You never would've dreamed of going to college before the war, but what the hell—with the GI Bill paying tuition, room and board, it's a great deal.

Except for these fraternity jerks in their letter sweaters. . . .

"Say there, aren't you a freshman?"

"That's right."

"You're supposed to be wearing your beanie."

"I bet I am."

Then you take away their girlfriends. You've got more money for dates, and girls know you're serious about getting married. By senior year, you're married to the former queen of the Tri-Delts and living in a converted garage with beaverboard walls and a deep-sink for the dishes, but it's home. The former Tri-Delt queen reads aloud from Fannie Hurst, the novelist: "A sleeping sickness is spreading among the women of the land. . . . They are retrogressing into . . . that thing known as The Home." You both get a laugh. But don't kid her about it, don't even think of saying anything like "A woman's place is in the home," or she'll brain you.

A raw, jagged feeling to things: bulldozers twitch across sad farms at the edge of town, cinder blocks rise out of cellar holes. William Levitt builds 17,447 houses on six thousand acres in four years. Children everywhere. Houses full of the fat stink of Mom's Toni home permanents and the scorched sawdust from Dad's basement hobby shop. Breezeways! Carports! Every Saturday another friend pulls into your driveway with a new little Crosley that looks like a Piper Cub without the wings, or a torpedo-back Chevy, or the fat, low Hudson that goes 120 miles an hour.

The critics, the intellectuals—they hate the suburbs but they like Jackie Robinson breaking the color line with the Brooklyn Dodgers. What they don't understand is that these things go together in America, it's all part of the same energy, two sides to everything.

You get a musical like *South Pacific*, about America ruling the world, and then you get a play like *Death of a Salesman* about the American Dream falling apart.

People say everybody hates Harry Truman. Then they reelect him.

Private life is everything, people keep saying. But if it's private, why do they keep saying it?

Picture windows! So people can look in and see your beautiful Christmas tree. Or your new television—the whole neighborhood drops by to see Milton Berle on the *Texaco Star Theater,* or Sugar Ray Robinson, the most beautiful fighter who ever lived, women love him.

You think about racism, communism . . . the world gets huge, the politics, the corporations where it's like the military. Wear a white shirt and be a team player, and if you don't mind moving all over the country you get promoted.

Everybody's moving up, everybody's middle class now. But people look at each other and say, "How long can it last?" The boom. The bomb. Loyalty oaths . . . crazy—you think a real Communist wouldn't just lie and sign the oath? Then the Russians set off an atom bomb years ahead of schedule, and the Communists take over China. Who the hell is responsible? Alger Hiss looks more and more like exactly the kind of upper-class creep who'd hand over secrets to the Reds.

There's a feeling that you can't take anything for granted anymore, you're not sure what to teach your children, except don't sit around in a wet bathing suit, that's how you get polio. The *Kinsey Report* comes out, saying we're all sexual deviates. You look at people at cocktail parties and you wonder, Are they doing that stuff? Am I missing something?

Cocktail parties! Whoever thought you'd be going to cocktail parties?

O beautiful, for spacious skies, for amber waves of grain that we keep sending to the starving Europeans no matter how much the New England chicken farmers complain. There's a feeling of fate in the air, good and bad, anything is possible, that's the message of the bomb, the United Nations, Judy Garland singing with that break-your-heart catch of amazement in her voice, *Life* magazine showing pictures of Jackson Pollock dripping housepaint on canvas and asking, "Is he the greatest living painter in the United States?"

If only it weren't for those goddamn Communists and the nightmare you can't get out of your mind after reading *1984* by George Orwell. Then again, do the Russians have a million television sets? Do they understand that it's Howdy Doody time?

It's like you're on a train that's not just speeding up but getting bigger and bigger in some infinite Einsteinian equation. Is it going to blow up? Is everybody on the train? Will we ever be able to get off?

The
Split-Level Years

. . . if you're just like everybody,
you're somebody . . .

S mell it, smell it all, smell the sour cities you leave behind in bosomy cars that smell of dusty sunlight and thump over Eisenhower's concrete interstate highways whose joints ooze tar that smells like industrial licorice till you arrive in a suburb smelling of insecticide and freshly cut grass outside identical houses full of the scents of postwar America: baked air hovering over the TV set; the mucilage on stickers for your art-appreciation course—*Mona Lisa, American Gothic,* the cozy stink of cigarette smoke freshened by Air-Wick deodorizer amid sweet pine paneling whose knots watch over you like the loving eyes of Disney forest creatures.

How sweet and new it all is, this incense of midcentury, this strange sense of coziness and infinite possibility at the same time.

Don't worry, Ike seems to say as he smiles and hits another

tee shot. You light another Camel, knowing that "It's a psychological fact: pleasure helps your disposition: For more pure pleasure—have a CAMEL."

There's a cartoon fullness to things. Everybody is somebody. Everything is possible. Hence a cushiony give in the national psyche, a pleasant ache that feels like nostalgia dispensed by a spray can. You believe in the future, be it a perfect marriage, racial integration, commuting via your personal autogiro, Formica countertops, or a day coming soon when everybody will be sincere and mature. ("Sincerity" and "maturity" are major virtues.)

Ignore the viruses of dread that float through family rooms: the hydrogen bomb erupting from the South Pacific like a cancerous jellyfish the size of God; or the evil Senator Joseph McCarthy and the evil Commies he never catches one of, not one, though he does manage to strew the land with damaged lives and the liberal tic of anti-anticommunism; or *Sputnik,* the first satellite, built by Russian slave labor, no doubt, while our top scientists were developing the Princess phone, 3-D movies, and boomerang-shaped coffee tables.

Ignore Marilyn Monroe saying, *What good is it being Marilyn Monroe? Why can't I just be an ordinary woman? . . . Oh, why do things have to work out so rotten?*

And ignore the Korean War, which is nothing but ugly except for the embroidered silk dragon jackets the soldiers bring back. Ignore the newspaper pictures of racists with faces like wet-combed hand grenades, screaming at Martin Luther King Jr.'s boycotters and schoolchildren who will overcome, people whose isolation and invisibility in this white society are incalculable. . . .

Progress will take care of everything.

Amid the Ford Country Squire station wagons and slate roofs, wealthier homeowners boast that neighborhood covenants still keep out Jews and Negroes. They offer you highballs and cigarettes. They show you black and white photographs of themselves waving from the rail of the *Queen Elizabeth*. They turn on lights till their houses blaze like cruise ships. What lonely darkness are they keeping off? Do they know their time has gone?

Meanwhile, amid the tract housing and developments, the genius of William Levitt and Henry Kaiser creates the loneliness of growing up in your own bedroom, in your own house where the green grass grows all around. It takes some getting used to, but do you really want to go back to the apartment with three kids to a bedroom and Nana mumbling over the cabbage? You know your future is here.

You wish you knew what it held.

"Children, your father's home!" Mom yells.

A father's Florsheim Imperials are heard. A Dobbs centerdent fedora is seen, with a jaunty trout-fly feather on the grosgrain band. Dad exudes the tired authority of cigarette smoke and Arrid underarm deodorant cream.

His knuckles whiten on a Christmas-present attaché case.

"Can't you kids get up off your duffs and do something instead of sitting there watching . . ."

"Hey, Dad's home."

". . . *Howdy Doody,* a little-children's show?"

"There's nothing else on, Dad."

Dad shouts over his shoulder, "Doris! You have any chores for these kids?"

"No, hon, everything's hunky-dory. You hungry?"

"Hell, yes, I'm hungry."

"Be dinner soon's I do the limas."

Sighing as if he has made a huge decision, Dad walks into the kitchen. He cracks ice for a drink.

"The kids," he says. "It's like I'm not even here."

"Well, it's like I always am," she says. "They're scared of you, but they take me for granted."

"Make you a drink?"

"Not too big, now."

His face struggles toward some home truth but doesn't find it.

"Ah, Doris," he says. "Turn off the stove and let's go to the Roma for veal scaloppine. Please. Just the two of us."

"I have to drop Tommy at Boy Scouts, and then Kitty Kennard is doing her slide show at L'Esprit Français. Forgive me?"

Doris and Tom Senior are only trying to live by what their parents taught them—manliness, graciousness, a day's work, good posture—and pass it on to their children. The problem is, they don't quite believe it themselves anymore, but they have to teach their kids *something*. Should they really confess their emptiness and bad faith instead? Should the children feel betrayed by parents who are only trying to do the best they know how?

How squalid. Let's leave all this behind. It's a symptom, not a cause, a failure when success is what you see on *Ozzie and Harriet* and all the other shows about breakfast-nook families where no one is taken for granted and everyone says hello. Hi, Rick. Hi, Pop. Hi, Dave. Good morning,

Mom. Dad's a bit of a bumbler, and what won't those darn kids think of next! Nevertheless, perfection is attainable. How smug one feels to know this. How inadequate one feels to know one hasn't attained it yet oneself, but one can put on a long-playing record of the perfect Ella Fitzgerald singing the Jerome Kern songbook perfectly.

Some of the young folks seem to have a hard time adjusting.

If I could have just one day when I wasn't all confused—if I felt I belonged someplace.
> —James Dean as the anguished son in
> *Rebel Without a Cause.*

Be part of progress like everybody else—the everybody you see on television and in *Life* magazine. Here's the equation: If you're just like everybody, then you're somebody. The way to be somebody is to buy something that makes you like everybody else who's bought the same thing—Ford owners reading their *Ford Times*es, Parliament smokers joined in aromatic sophistication. Remember, consumption is a moral good. Madison Avenue admen are cultural heroes, with cool slang like "Let's run it up the flagpole and see who salutes."

Look at all the college kids stuffing themselves into phone booths and Volkswagens. And the lovely girl whose picture appears in *Life* next to the comment, "She has forgotten all about emancipation and equality. To belong is her happiness."

And Mary Ann Cuff, a regular among the teen dancers who appear on Dick Clark's *American Bandstand:* "What it is we all want is to get married and live on the same street in new houses. We'll call it Bandstand Avenue."

Ignore the hipsters and intellectuals sneering at Bandstand Avenue and at the triumphalism of tail fins, *Time* magazine, and pointy bras whose tips crinkle under sweaters.

Sure, fun can be made of bomb shelters stocked with Franco-American canned spaghetti and Reader's Digest Condensed Books.

J. D. Salinger can appeal to adolescent self-righteousness by railing against phonies in *The Catcher in the Rye.* Scorn can be heaped on Ray Kroc, who runs those new McDonald's drive-ins; he writes in a memo, "We cannot trust some people who are nonconformist. The organization cannot trust the individual, the individual must trust the organization." And certainly critics can make a living by attacking the men in the gray flannel suits, the organization men, the lonely crowd of ulcer-proud hidden persuaders bringing us ads where women in crinoline-fluffed shirtwaists invite us to buy into the carefree new patio-perfect world of hyperpower Torque-flite Cyclamatic Teletouch Whatever that gives you more pleasure. (Repeat through fade-out: MORE PLEASURE! MORE PLEASURE! MORE PLEASURE!)

Which does not mean sex, boys and girls.

Sex is for Europeans, people in movies (offscreen), and juvenile delinquents. White people believe that colored people have sex lives of unimaginable ecstasy and variety. Italian kids drive surly Mercurys to the Jersey Shore, spread blankets, and neck in Ace-combed 1953 look-at-me majesty beneath the outraged stares of moms in bathing suits with little skirts—prefiguring the erotic insolence of Elvis, Marilyn, James Dean, and the secret subtext of Annette Funicello on *The Mickey Mouse Club*.

Otherwise, sex, the lonely vandal, is safe in the stewardship of middle-class women who manage the courtship rituals of dating, going steady, pinning, and engagement, and aren't very interested in sex anyway, according to *Life* magazine's establishment take on the *Kinsey Report on Women*. "Woman is the placid gender, the female guppy swimming all unconcerned and wishing she could get a few minutes off to herself, while the male guppy pursues her with his unrelenting courtship. . . . Half or more of all women . . . seldom dream or daydream about sex; they consider the human body to be, if anything, rather repulsive."

Maybe men make cracks about women's driving and spending, and they want dinner served on time, but *Life* has learned that the unrelenting guppy is becoming the "new American domesticated male" who is "baby tender, dishwasher, cook, repairman. . . . Some even go to baby-care classes, learn to wrap a neat diaper and to bubble Junior deftly. With father available as sitter, wives can have their hair done, shop, go to club meetings." Lawn mowing gives him "a sense of power and a gadget to tinker with."

What happened to the red-blooded, can-do, all-American male? And female?

Well, sexed women and powerful men are a threat. We don't need them now. Passion has been replaced by love, adventure by fun. If you want sex, watch Elvis Presley on the *Ed Sullivan Show,* even if Ed refuses to show the King below the waist. Or go to a movie starring Marilyn Monroe or Ava Gardner. If you want male brooding and rage, go see Marlon Brando or Montgomery Clift, the prince of loneliness.

The great thing about the fifties is that rebels can throw

their bombs of anger and irony into the cafés of the con-
formists, safe in the knowledge that they can't really change
anything. The fifties are an irresistible force still in search of
an immovable object.

So pay no attention to that slouching bohemian with sunglasses black as telephones and a tremor induced by his Ben-
zedrine inhaler. He says he wants to get back to Europe,
"where they really know how to live, where they don't have
these hang-ups."

"Europe?" asks the astonished corporate executive who
helped liberate Europe from the Nazis only a decade or so
ago. "You can't even drink the water in Europe."

"You drink wine, man," says the bohemian. "You drink
wine."

Don't worry about snooty intellectuals, either. For a
moment, a Columbia University professor named Charles
Van Doren is a national celebrity on a big-money TV quiz
show called *Twenty-One*. He appears on the cover of *Time*.
He seems to be the answer to the old American question "If
you're so smart, why aren't you rich?" Then it turns out the
producers are slipping him the answers to keep him on the
show.

Van Doren is disgraced, treated like a traitor for lying on television. Well, intellectuals. It just goes to show you. They're all homos or Commies anyway.

And don't worry about the alienation of the modern jazz that lures college boys to the big city for a taste of hip, and the self-loathing notion that "white cats don't swing."

Don't worry about rock and roll, which sounds like a national anthem for the republic of vandalism and anarchy—which it is. Rock may drive the young folk to drugs and groin-thrusting madness, it may cause riots in the streets and insurrection in the schools—which it does—but it can't last, it's just a fad.

Ignore the sly joke of Frankie Lymon and the Teenagers singing "No, no, no, no, no, I'm not a juvenile delinquent" to suburban kids who actually think JDs are cool in their rumbles fought with bicycle chains and switchblade knives. So cool that Leonard Bernstein, Mr. Music Appreciation Class himself, will write *West Side Story,* a musical that puts romantic love and gang wars together in a climactic switch-blade duel.

Forget about civil-rights workers heading south, where they're known as northern agitators. And the revival of pinko folk singers like Pete Seeger and the Weavers. And marijuana in Harvard Square. And Hugh Hefner proposing in *Playboy* magazine that we should think of sex as fun, like a game of picnic badminton where nobody tries too hard to win.

"There's a place for us," the cast sings at the end of *West Side Story*, to reassure us that despite the tragedy of Tony and Maria, the promise of progress is intact. "Someday, somewhere, we'll find a new way of living."

There are no VA mortgages for veterans of gang wars, but America will find a way to get them into little Cape Cod starter homes sooner than you might think. Haircuts, briefcases, Peter Pan blouses, Formica, Bisquick and pole lamps, while the whole family sits in front of the television to sing along with Mitch:

"I'm looking over a four-leaf clover . . ."

How could it be otherwise?

Everything Possible, Nothing Real

. . . what could go wrong . . .

Yeah, sure, why not, cool, c'mon in, crash with me for the night, knock and it shall be opened unto you, ask and ye shall receive.

But who knocked? Who asked? Which one among you can recall your personal version of the 1960s and say you seized all the opportunities laid out across the psychic landscape of America like cocaine on the mirrored nightstand of a girl you hadn't been introduced to because there just wasn't time?

You missed it.

Who rode the stock-market run-up? Who got laid? Who shivered with a velveteen mouth and camouflage eyes in the predawn tree-line funk of Phu Bai? Who hung out at (————) when (————) was still hanging out there? Who surfed? Frugged with kohl-rimmed apathy at Maxwell's Plum? Rode south with the Freedom Riders? Thought

America could save its soul with its mind—its Kennedy White House cello concerts, its Harvard LSD mysticism, its sexual mystery plays? (Regardless of the fact that saving a soul with a mind is like fixing a leak with a bucket.)

Few, few, few of us.

Who was "booted, pantsuited, birth-controlled and pleasure-goaled," as Gail Sheehy wrote of the women in New York singles bars . . . soldiers in the sexual revolution, all the Mustang Sallys who lived in Torrance, California, and went to courtyard-apartment pool parties in frilled bikinis?

And boys who jacked up the backs of 409 Chevys, mounted cheater-slick tires, and installed blower scoops that sucked the astonished oxygen out of the lungs of every small-town kid in America?

And how many girls wore a Mary Quant / Twiggy / go-go dancer miniskirt so short you had to practice getting in and out of a car?

And who got stoned for the first of a thousand times and realized that air is, like, a thing . . . like you move through it, man, and it's cool on your forehead and the back of your hands as if you had a fever and . . . what is that music?

And O sad-eyed lady of Bloomington, Indiana, whatever

happened to the boy with the long, long hair the color of a cocoa-butter tan and the knack for making you believe that anything you gave him was a gift he'd never been given before? And years later, why in God's name did you think of him in the middle of your bar exam?

You missed it.

Even in the middle of the fun or the craziness, you kept feeling like a by-product for which there was no product, like the side effect of a drug somebody else had taken, the effect being the sense that something had been right there, right in the palm of your hand like a baby bird, and then it tried to fly and the cat got it.

The thing was, you should have been there last night/ last month/last year before it got ruined, commercialized, co-opted by the pigs, back when it was really the Rolling Stones, a commune, Mississippi, the Peace Corps, the revolution, back when you still needed four-wheel drive to get there, before the rip-off artists showed up acting like they invented the goddam electric guitar/sit-in/lotus position/ orgy/ American Indian/Peace Corps/New Hampshire primary/ geodesic dome/rock festival/boycott.

Bummer.

It's time to call my old Marine buddy Peter Dunne. He lives in New Jersey and answers the phone for a car-alarm company.

Like me, he hates nostalgia, so talking with him is like a tongue searching for a sore tooth, then playing with it for laughs.

"Here's a weird thing," I say. "I hated being in Vietnam. But about a year after we got back, I started having this terrible yearning to be back there. Even when I started demonstrating against the war. It was like I didn't do enough, like at Chu Lai we got attacked with grenades and rifle fire but I should've gotten under rocket fire—"

"Like you should've gotten wounded," Peter says.

"Christ, I guess," I say.

He says, "When I got hit, I'm coming up out of the water in the paddy, I'm alive, and I'm saying, 'Good, good, good, it's a wound, I'm going home.' And I never wanted to go back. It was so strange, I'm sitting there with blood all over and the first thing I see is Domville—remember Domville?—and before he helps me, he stands back and takes my picture, and later on he sends it to me in the hospital. Why did he do that?"

"He wanted to make sure he didn't miss it," I say. "Or you didn't miss it."

He says, "I try to tell people about the sixties, but my memory is like a book that got burned, and what's left is charred ovals of pages, and they're out of order."

I say, "But there are moments, like you never forget where you were when you heard Kennedy was shot."

"I was on some ship, debarking at Okinawa, humping all our equipment, in line for hours. Somebody says Kennedy got shot, we all thought it was Sergeant Kennedy in C Company, we said, 'Good, somebody got that mother.'"

"I saw John Kennedy in 1960," I say.

"Great. Was it cool?" he asks, with the tiny tang of irony one picked up in Vietnam.

"I was working as a dishwasher on Cape Cod, and he flew back to Hyannis after he got nominated. We met the plane. He got off and he just looked like an actor to me, like he had makeup on—"

"And nothing behind it," Peter says.

"Later, after he got killed and everybody's so worked up about it, I wondered if I'd missed something. I'd think maybe I should've joined the Peace Corps. Then I'd run into Peace

Corps volunteers just back from Botswana or someplace, and they were completely out of it, no idea what was happening with dope, music, the war, politics. . . ."

Peter says, "I could've gone to Haight-Ashbury, the Summer of Love, but I didn't. I went out to Chicago for the riots during the Democratic Convention in '68. It was great, but I'd be in a riot and I'd know there was a cooler riot going on in another part of the city."

"You got to Woodstock," I say. "I missed it—sleeping on the ground, the rain. It sounded too much like the Marines."

"It was great. I did acid. I got naked."

"And then the Hell's Angels killed that guy at Altamont, with the Rolling Stones. I mean, if Woodstock was so great, how come we couldn't have more of them?"

"I thought things would change," Peter says. "I thought we could make people peaceful, we were going to change mankind, and then you see you're getting ripped off by the manipulators, SDS, Joan Baez marrying David Somebody because he was going to jail and that made them both cool. You remember *Be Here Now?* That thing from Baba Ram Dass, the guy who did LSD at Harvard with Timothy Leary? I believed that. It messed me up for four years, that's what my working in the gas station for all those years was about. I didn't take hold of my life; I was being here now. Or acid: you bought into it, you thought you were going to have a revelation that would change everything, and then you didn't."

What made the sixties great was the fifties-fostered belief that Everything Was Possible. For a few years there at the beginning, it seemed so easy, like one of those dreams where you discover how to fly—you just arch your back just so, nothing to it—no heroism necessary, enjoyed where prohibited, just consume, consume, consume: sex, sports cars, ecstasy, Bermuda shorts, enlightenment, Playboy Bunnies, bare feet in the park, stereos, freedom, justice, truth, art . . . a pastel ease to things. Oh, smell the new smells of nondairy creamer, tear gas, marijuana, Tang, Cool Whip, sand-candle-lit sex, button-tufted Naugahyde car interiors, dormitory cat pee, and sandalwood incense; hear the cool rustle of beanbag chairs, the I-think-I-can whirring of VW Microbuses climbing the Continental Divide.

There was the Cuban missile crisis, and people kept getting assassinated: Malcolm X, Bobby Kennedy, Martin Luther King Jr., civil-rights workers. But those things seemed like mere accidents at first. We had a right to happiness, as if it were something we could demand, like the vote . . . a wild joke on the old Depression-head Larry Lunchpails also known as Dad . . . while the background music had the lotus-land melancholy of "California Dreamin'" by the Mamas and the Papas, or "Ooh, Baby, Baby," by Smokey Robinson and the Miracles, who slid through your mind like a lost kite drifting down the beach, this being early in the sixties, when musicians still smiled and bowed when they performed (except for Bob Dylan, who always had the poignancy and anger, the possibility and paranoia working together).

What could go wrong?

Science and liberalism had repudiated the notion of the innate depravity of mankind, so every little baby-boom baby was pure, innocent, and perfect.

John Kennedy would wipe out stodginess. Then Lyndon Johnson said: "The Great Society rests on abundance and liberty for all. It demands an end to poverty and racial injustice. But that is just the beginning."

I drove south in 1962, back when the South was filled with people who despised me or craved my approval. Times were changing. Everybody knew it. There was a high subliminal tremor to things, as if you were looking at an abandoned child whose only toy was its father's bowie knife. Too much was possible. I left a few weeks too early to see James Meredith integrate the University of Mississippi, and I completely missed the inevitability that it would be the North, not the South, that was going to explode in all its Yankee sanctimony: Burn, baby, burn. In 1965, when the Los Angeles neighborhood of Watts blew up, the black Marines I knew stopped acknowledging my presence when they walked past in groups.

Clearly, I had missed something.

Of course, if you were black, you didn't have to worry about missing it because it was happening everywhere, the sit-ins early on and the Black Power later, with long hot summers of riots being either fact or fear (or hope, until the bodies were counted) in cities across the country—not to mention that for all those years your self and authenticity weren't something you had to go looking for in the manner of some Princeton kid hitchhiking to Vermont with his dog named Mr. Natural. Because every time you woke up and walked out the door it was the white man's America and Something Was on the Line. You didn't even have to think about it.

You just may have believed there was a glamour to be found in the company of the beautiful young gunmen known as the Black Panthers. And the long-lost continent of Africa arose as homeland and Eden. And either you'd read Frantz Fanon's *Wretched of the Earth* or you hadn't—it was a consciousness thing.

Or, black or white, maybe you missed all of this sort of sixties, the decade that the documentaries are about, from acid to Maharishi Mahesh Yogi to shoot-outs.

Look at high school yearbooks, even college yearbooks, from the sixties. Where are the hippies and the revolutionaries? Forget it. What you see is page after page of the future dentists of America, the kindergarten teachers, aluminum-siding salesmen, and cops, guys who went to Playboy Clubs, kids who went to work with Dad in his plumbing and heating business, who thought Frank Sinatra and the Rat Pack were cool, who didn't notice that John Wayne masculinity was going out of fashion, who didn't have any idea what the Beatles meant when they sadly sang

I read the news today oh boy
About a lucky man who made the grade

Ah, the news. It just added to the notion that everything was possible and nothing was quite real.

Starting with John Kennedy's funeral, the news became drama. The heroes of Vietnam were correspondents, not soldiers. Walter Cronkite was more important than any astronaut he ever covered. Reality became entertainment, turning Americans from citizens into critics. The rising media-political class actually believed that television had brought the war and everything else into its living rooms. When they heard you'd been in Vietnam, they'd say, "Isn't the *Times* doing a wonderful job? Did you see that series on NBC?"

Such comfy folly.

The sixties have never ended for some people, but for most they lasted as long as you could imagine that the bad news was just a freak: the killings of King, Bobby Kennedy, the students at Kent State and Jackson State, the rioters in Newark, Detroit, Washington. . . . When King was killed, I remember a TV station in New York whose coverage consisted of the camera fixed on one word handwritten on a white card: SHAME. That was the news, that day.

Finally, there were so many possibilities floating around

that either nobody was a freak or everybody was, from Richard Nixon with his face like a biopsy sample to Allen Ginsberg coyly swaddled in the irony of his nineteenth-century-bard beard and Uncle Sam–hat. I recall reading about deb-party drunks in white tie singing World War I songs at the Plaza Hotel—the old WASP anthems—the same night the Rolling Stones checked in, each group no doubt trying to figure out which was the native, which the raj.

The Syllogism of the Sixties: When everything is possible, nothing is real. When nothing is real, everything is folly. When everything is folly, things turn nasty with ulterior motives, opportunism, psychopaths, acid burnouts, and radical politicians who smoke dope and dig Hendrix and all, but then they start laying this stuff on you about Marcuse's concept of repressive tolerance and how killing cops is an act of liberation. From Nixon to some sixteen-year-old getting high in his basement, the working paradigm was paranoia.

Total paranoia is total awareness, said Charlie Manson, the Hollywood butcher-guru, but he was wrong. It's also the militant wing of self-pity, of which there was a lot when sixties America ended up in the liberation quagmire of which Vietnam was only the saddest part.

It began with a first joint, demonstration, surfboard, whatever. The medium was the message. It ended when you were overwhelmed by a sense of psychic disenfranchisement.

Anyway, it's your sixties. Feel free to start and end it whenever you choose.

The joke of it all turned into self-righteous vandalism, the smashing of bank windows and all. You got older. You had to stop acting like children when you started having them. There was anger and chagrin. Cocaine replaced flower-painted cheeks with eyes full of power-trip condescension.

Or, as we started to say at the end of an era that began with such grace, hope, and fun: Heavy . . . heavvvvYYYYY.

1970–1980

Heavy

. . . stayin' alive, stayin' alive . . .

I t's, like, the seventies.

    It's like . . . what . . . like soggy, like a sinus condition, the kind that makes your head so heavy it droops like a peony.

    Lotta drugs, lotta sex, lotta therapy, hugging and polyester clothing with a stiff, sticky feeling . . . the big Frye boots with rings on the ankles, the hatch-cover coffee tables, the ponderous melancholy of lite and heavy rock (Fleetwood Mac, Black Sabbath), the vans with the neo–Frank Frazetta paintings on the sides showing saber-toothed tigers being ridden by chicks with proto-exploding breasts . . . *Saturday Night Fever* with the disco soundtrack that becomes a kind of motto: *Stayin' alive, stayin' alive.* . . .

    Heavy.

    Plenty of stuff happens in the seventies—Watergate, the helicopters lifting refugees from the roof of our embassy in

Saigon, the Iran hostage crisis, the Chevette rolling off the line to become celebrated as America's least-stolen car—but it feels like every locomotive in America is rusted to the rails, like the karmic ice cream spoon is stuck to the bottom of the cosmic bowl, like the fifties and sixties were the irresistible force and now the seventies are the immovable object.

It's like a TV show you've never seen before but it feels like a rerun, something wrong with the laugh track.

It's like being stuck in a 3 A.M. bus station with nothing to read but the answer page to a lost magazine quiz. The answers are: near-meltdown at Three Mile Island, Comet Kohoutek, gas shortage, the former Republic of South Vietnam, oil spills, two million Cambodians, depletion of the ozone layer, Elvis Presley (in his bathroom), Muslim fundamentalists, endangered Furbish lousewort, Legionnaires' disease in air-conditioning systems, serial murder, Johnny Rotten and the Sex Pistols, Patty Hearst and the Symbionese Liberation Army, blaxploitation movies, a million PCB-contaminated eggs, failed hostage rescue, wage and price controls, hundreds with cyanide in Jonestown.

The speed of the sixties steams down to the matter of the

seventies. *Do* becomes *is*. The chicken fat of American culture coagulates in the refrigerator darkness.

It's 10:43 on Saturday night in the casino, and somebody's hair is on fire.

"You smell something burning?" says a girl in platform shoes, with hair curled back on the sides in Farrah Fawcett wings.

"I can't smell anything," her boyfriend says, without taking the cigar out of his mouth. He wears a Qiana shirt with chest hair erupting like an ascot, hair like the stuff in furnace filters.

They're waiting for the lounge singer to come back and sing "Feelings" again.

They talk without looking at each other. They look out instead at the dawnless acres of a casino, six thousand people working away at slot machines and craps tables as if this were a factory, but a factory where they don't pay you to work, you pay them. *Stayin' alive, stayin' alive....* A sense of dark, futile momentum, along with paranoia, as if you were being watched every minute, which you are, through those one-way hemisphere mirrors in the ceiling. This is the feeling of the seventies—the feeling of being watched, the mild ache of self-consciousness like being high on marijuana, the feeling of the liberated, therapy-grouped you looking in the mirror and seeing a yellow happy-face sticker that says "Have a Nice Day."

"Like hair burning," the girl says.

"Like nothing," he says. "After all that nose candy upstairs, how can you smell anything?"

"That stuff doesn't do anything for me," she says.

"So I noticed."

"What, I'm supposed to get all undressed so we can make love with runny noses?"

"You want the swingers to have all the fun?" he asks. "You should hear the guys at the store talk, what goes on. They got orgies going on, is what. They got a place in New York, Plato's Retreat, and one called Sandstone in California. Pretty soon it'll be everywhere, like miniature golf."

"They got orgies, the rest of us are lining up for gas," says the girlfriend. "The president of the United States turned out to be a crook, the Viet Cong are running the American Embassy, my sister is going out with a married guy, my brother is going out with a married guy."

"Hey, if it feels good, do it," the boyfriend says.

"I smell it."

"Maybe it's your bra on fire, all this women's lib you talk."

"That never happened, that bra burning," she says. "That's a male-chauvinist myth."

"First they get rid of their bras," he says, "then they find out men love this no-bra look, so they get back in bras. Or a couple years ago, a man could get lynched for saying a woman's mood might change once a month or so. Then this woman kills somebody and she says it's because she has the curse, and all the women's-lib groups back her up."

"We don't say 'the curse' anymore."

"Everything changes names. The Indians are all Native Americans now, and the disadvantaged turned into the handicapped—or vice versa, I can't keep up."

"Great," she says. "I go away for the weekend and I end up on *All in the Family*. A date with Archie Bunker. Next thing you'll be talking about the Hebes and the spades."

"You wanted *The Brady Bunch? Mary Tyler Moore?*" he asks. "You want to bounce around with big smiles, be my guest."

"I went out with this jerk, he tried to take me to see *Deep Throat*."

"You go?"

"I already seen it. He wants me to see it again, like I didn't get the idea the first time. I made him take me to see *Star Wars* instead. Now there's a movie. All the other movies nowadays take everything apart. Like *Jaws* or *The Godfather* show you how rotten things are. Disaster movies. *Star Wars* puts everything together. I can't explain. But like, I want to be Princess Leia."

"You want to know my life's ambition?" he asks. "I never told anybody this. I want one shot on the *Tonight Show*, just one. It's crazy, but I think about it. I come out, sit down, Johnny Carson says, 'So how do you get into the major-appliance business?' And I say, 'You start out in minor appliances.' That's my joke, right? Because, like, there's no such thing as a minor—"

"I'm laughing, I'm dying," she says. "Why don't you try out for *Dean Martin's Celebrity Roast?*"

"I smell it now," the boyfriend says.

"Your cigar," she says.

"What I paid for this cigar, it better not smell like hair burning."

"No," she says. "It's sparks falling on your chest."

"Hey, a forest fire," he says, swatting at the smoldering triangle of hair.

"What a man," she says.

"At least I didn't put any holes in the shirt—I got it from the same guy did Travolta's costumes in *Saturday Night Fever*."

They stare out at the casino, the great factory where the raw material is human folly and the end product is a thrill or two but mostly disappointment.

"What it is, you used to expect to win in this country," the girl says.

"And now," he says, "you just try to lose slow enough that you can stay in the casino."

Stayin' alive. . . .

We blew it. We were going to save the soul of America.

Then we lose in Vietnam, OPEC shuts off our oil, President Nixon resigns, the economy goes south. People wander in the smog of aftermath and say, "It's like the blessing has been removed from our land."

President Carter says, "Two problems of our country—energy and malaise."

It's like being trapped in a full-body cast and your only

connection with the world is a CB radio where Henry Kissinger reads to you from *Gravity's Rainbow* . . . like the whole decade has an adenoid problem . . . like your brain is a lava lamp or your lava lamp is a brain.

Industry turns into the Rust Belt. The military goes into a nervous breakdown. Respect declines for male muscle and the work ethic. Respect rises for female sensitivity, education, and, most of all, victimhood. Anybody who's anybody is a victim now. Except for heterosexual white males, unless they're screwed-up Vietnam veterans. (And by the time the media get through, every last one of them will look screwed up.)

Divorce becomes just another rite of passage on the road to freedom, the rate rising from 2.5 per thousand Americans in 1965 to 5.2 in 1980. Parents don't stick together for the sake of the children, they get divorced for the sake of the children, saying, "Better they should have one happy parent than two miserable ones."

Or better to have no children at all, a notion encouraged among the highly educated by movies such as *Rosemary's Baby* and *The Exorcist*.

"I'm a partner at Meadham, Munch—and you?" asks the bright young woman at the party.

"I take care of my two children," says the other woman.

"Well, I'm sure you feel very lucky," says the bright young woman. "I don't know anyone who has children now. I look at the population figures around the world, and somehow I'd feel so guilty having children, I think. Garrett and I have talked about adopting a Third World child, but finding someone to take care of it is so hard."

"Have you thought of buying a golden retriever instead?" asks the mother of two.

Selfishness trickles down to the leisure-suit set as a philosophic principle.

"Get mine, baby," says an ad salesman on the elevator.

"Taking care of Number One," says another salesman.

"If you don't, who will?" asks the first salesman.

It's like the whole world has been injection-molded in off-orange and chestnut vinyl, as if everything is an imitation of itself, every sideburn, shag rug, Buick LeSabre, giraffe-pattern throw pillow.

A countermovement fights for authenticity. It installs Vermont Castings wood stoves in houses with perfectly good central heating, wears wood-soled Swedish exercise shoes, shingles its kitchen walls, and gives its children unpainted unisex hand-carved wooden toys that match the furniture.

Country-and-western music, with its tales of weathered men and stoic women, gets popular with people who are neither. (Both sides listen to Bruce Springsteen, who is heralded as the future of rock and roll and almost is.)

Authenticity versus imitation: a century of philosophic debate dwindles to a set of life-style consumer choices in the name of self-actualization, self-esteem, self-discovery.

"From 1971 to 1975, I directly experienced est, Gestalt therapy, bioenergetics, Rolfing, massage, jogging, health foods, t'ai chi, Esalen, hypnotism, modern dance, meditation, Silva Mind Control, Arica, acupuncture, sex therapy, Reichian therapy—a smorgasbord course in New Consciousness," says Jerry Rubin, the sixties street radical who ends up as a Wall Street securities analyst.

You no longer practice politics or espouse a philosophy; instead you explore what sort of victimhood you suffer for being gay, female, black, Latino, Native American, old, poor, insane, crippled, vegetarian. . . .

Stayin' alive, stayin' alive. . . .

In *The Culture of Narcissism,* Christopher Lasch argues, "In a dying culture, narcissism appears to embody—in the guise of personal 'growth' and 'awareness'—the highest attainment of spiritual enlightenment. The custodians of culture hope, at bottom, merely to survive its collapse."

Dying culture! Collapse! Bye, bye, Miss American Pie!

Nearly every one of us, nearly every day of his life, is contributing directly to the ruin of this planet. . . . The mentality that exploits and destroys the natural environment is the same that abuses racial and economic minorities.

—Wendell Berry, poet, essayist, ecologist, farmer, lecturer

Spaceship Earth is now filled to capacity or beyond and is running out of food. . . . Thermonuclear bombs, poison gases and super-germs have been manufactured and stockpiled by people in the few first-class compartments.

—Paul Ehrlich, author of *The Population Bomb*

Not only nature but humankind has turned against us. What happened to the doctrine of human progress? What happened to nature being our friend? Where oh where are Walt Disney's bluebirds to bring us lunch in beribboned baskets now that we're lost in the forest that merely seemed like a sunny primrose path a few years ago? And what about nature's happiest harbinger of them all, formerly known as the sexual revolution but now plagued with diseases you never even heard of before: herpes, chlamydia. . . .

Why, O Princess Leia, are we pursued across the universe by defeat, running sores, music that sounds like a factory floor of drop-forges with strobe lights . . . by the Dark Side of the Force?

Morning Again

. . . greed is healthy . . .

This is the Air Guitar Decade.

People aren't themselves, they're the roles they play. Things don't have to be things, just be *like* things: authentic imitation bomber jackets, suburban country kitchens with the Martha Stewart baskets that never carry anything . . . Martha Stewart herself, in fact—the air-guitar perfection of Martha as mom, hostess, gardener, and chef . . . she's an idea in people's minds, like Donald Trump playing Donald Trump and building buildings he can put "Trump" on. (He gets called "The People's Billionaire" by the *New York Daily News*. That's the kind of decade it is.)

"I'm not a doctor, but I play one on TV," says a soap-opera actor who does an ad for Vicks cough syrup as if he were the top upper-respiratory man at Johns Hopkins.

An actor is elected president. Talking to a journalist who

mistakenly recalls seeing him on a movie set, Ronald Reagan says, "You believed in it because you wanted to believe it. There's nothing wrong with that. I do it all the time."

Previous presidents have played the hero, but Reagan understands that the presidency of the eighties is a character role, requiring a character actor's coy opacity—a face like folk art, simple and sturdy, a cameo carved in a walnut shell, a face so familiar you seem to see every detail even at a distance: the 1940s hair he never changed (that wave mounting back from his forehead, a reverse of Kennedy's mop), the chevron tilt to the eyes, the preoccupied alertness of the nearsighted, the glance of the slightly deaf, sharp and meek at the same time. His mouth puckers in an unhurried O and then a smile slides to the side of his face while he arches an eyebrow—the jaunty but purposeful look of a man who looks like he's got his hat cocked to one side even when he isn't wearing a hat.

Symbol is substance everywhere.

Witch hunts—literally—ruin the lives of day-care workers. Altar orgies! Satanism! (Are we feeling guilty about handing our children over to strangers on our way to work? Is that what this craziness symbolizes?) The media get very serious about the Iran-contra scandal, but it looks more like an air-guitar Watergate. The homeless represent America's callousness, but it turns out that many aren't homeless as much as they're schizophrenic or alcoholic.

The symbolism of taking up combat positions might hurt our diplomacy in Lebanon, so Marines are ordered to bunk down in an office building where a suicide bomber kills 241 of them. Days later, this setback is symbolically redeemed by our victory over a Caribbean country called Grenada, which has gotten too cozy with Cuba and communism for our liking.

The New Hampshire schoolteacher-citizen-mom Christa McAuliffe isn't a scientist or an astronaut, but she gets to ride on the *Challenger* space shuttle for 73.621 seconds as Mrs. Front Porch USA in Space. Then it blows up.

Reagan gets the news. He asks, "That's the one the teacher's on?"

Some news is not so symbolic. There are recessions and firings, drug-driven crime turning cities into free-fire zones. Reagan gets shot. The pope gets shot. Airplanes blow up, and people are afraid to travel. Your kindly hometown savings and loan collapses, and you, the taxpayer, have to make good on its debts. AIDS is going to kill everybody if we don't do something.

After some patches of early-eighties fog, Reagan announces, "It's morning again in America."

Not dawn's early light, maybe, but a placid ten-thirty or so, with "Doc down at the drugstore thinking about pulling the skin books off the magazine rack, the fifty-five-mile-an-hour speed limit a thing of Jimmy Carter's age-of-limits past, the school kids back to basics, and most people back to work," as a media type writes.

The Cold War ends. The chattering classes have a hard time giving credit to Reagan, but it happened on his watch. America shrugs off a stock-market crash. There's a conditional stability to things, like the feeling when you walk toward the baggage claim after a bumpy plane ride. Things feel larger than life and unreal at the same time, a condition Jean Baudrillard calls hyperreality. (He's a French intellectual—they've gotten very big again.) Experience is a theme park, reality sings through a karaoke microphone, and authenticity is a brand name on your shirt, sneakers, blazer, purse. Those aren't underpants, those are Calvin Kleins. That isn't three days' growth of beard, you're just doing Don Johnson from *Miami Vice*.

Cocaine is the psychic vitamin of the moment. It turns existence itself into an air guitar, as if you can become an idea of yourself. Cocaine makes you feel famous, gives you an edgy hyperclarity, as if you were looking at yourself through the wrong end of the binoculars. Airless, wary, presumptuous—this is the founding mood of postmodernism, which is to say self-consciousness. Not a painful self-consciousness, but a feeling of being a Peeping Tom looking through your own window. It's a short step to the exhibitionism of televised confession on the Phil Donahue and Geraldo Rivera shows, or to the upscale trend-toadies replacing their curtains with "window treatments" that let passersby see them sitting on chintz couches petting a Lhasa apso as if they were practicing for Robin Leach's *Lifestyles of the Rich and Famous.* Except the Lhasa apso keeps peeing on the rug (they have an appointment with the pet psychologist to work on this).

The personal is the political, as if private and public lives were the same, nothing to hide and nothing to tell. The ideal for these people is to live at one pleasant remove from reality, as if they were touring another country, drinking bottled water and sampling food from each other's plate while the waiters talk about them. They fill the rest of their time by working eighty-two-hour weeks, then standing in movie lines and asking their friends what happened on *Miami Vice* or *Hill Street Blues*.

The response: "All I watch is MTV. I start watching some horrible video from Twisted Sister or somebody and I'm hooked."

You jog in your jogging clothes, lift weights in your weight-lifting clothes, and look at yourself in the mirror as if you were auditioning to be your own body double. Sweet pain, cruel pleasure. Arnold Schwarzenegger and Sly Stallone inspire men to grow breasts at the gym. Women "go for the burn" with Jane Fonda's workout tapes. They burn off so much body fat that they stop having periods. Air-guitar sexiness.

Air guitar: as in kids in their rooms playing phantom guitars and duplicating every last Bruce Springsteen wince of astonishment and leap of sweaty ecstasy while a boom box hammers out "Born in the USA." Or Guns N' Roses mime-bands of high school talent-show kids raging through "Welcome to the Jungle," hurling hands, hair, and groins around with evil triumphalism.

Air guitar gets so big it becomes a movie bit: Tom Cruise in *Risky Business* does "Old Time Rock and Roll" in his underpants, using a trophy for a microphone. The bit makes both the movie and Tom Cruise, who plays an eighties-bred greedhead kid portrayed as a hero for blackmailing his way into Princeton.

He's an air-guitar kind of guy, when you think about it—one of those ambitious, well-handled, career-driven eighties actors who don't play characters as much as they play successful actors playing characters, like Kathleen Turner, Michael Douglas, and Harrison Ford. Unlike the stars who are dying off—Bette Davis, Cary Grant, Fred Astaire—the new generation makes it look hard instead of easy, the work ethic as work aesthetic.

Wall Street hustlers become heroes of the new capitalism not only because they work so hard and get so rich but also because they've learned how to turn work directly into money without the grubby middleman business of making things like cars or clothes—why bother? If you want to make money, just make money by manipulating money, wallowing in it like Scrooge McDuck diving into his comic-book pile of gold coins. "Greed is healthy!" Ivan Boesky tells Berkeley business students three years before he goes to prison. "You can be greedy and still feel good about yourself."

Michael Jackson makes his megamillions by cutting out the middleman of artistic soul and becoming his audience's expectations, with the haunted face of too much plastic surgery and a collection of clever moves: the single glitter glove, the moonwalk. He doesn't dance so much as he presents a series of nifty gestures, in the manner of a particularly deft store clerk wrapping himself up as a birthday present to himself.

Jesse Jackson becomes a national political figure without ever holding office. Why bother? Just do the photo ops, the press conferences, the disaster visits, the head-of-state conferences.

Fame seems almost a right, a need, a psychological food group. It comes in various intensities, from victimhood as portrayed in *People* magazine to the air-guitar notoriety of a singer named Madonna. She writhes around onstage in her underwear singing, "I am just a material girl, living in a material world." But she isn't. She's just an idea in the minds of teenage girls, and of assistant professors who write essays about her in language like "the deployment of difference in the tactical form of gender pastiche . . . shifts the quality and meaning of resistance to institutionalized heteromasculinity."

Nothing material about her at all: Madonna is a fictional character without an author. She creates herself. Madonna becomes "Madonna."

How nice. We don't have to take these people very seriously, but we can enjoy their performances. How comfortable.

In the same way, Tama Janowitz writes novels—*Slaves of New York*, for instance—so she can become "Tama Janowitz." She is quite famous.

"You see Tama Janowitz doing that vodka ad in the magazine, her and that older guy?" asks a bond trader. He's eating dinner at Portobello with a decorator who got a spread in *W* for doing whole apartments in taupe.

"I think I bought her book," says the decorator. "Or maybe it was by Elizabeth Tallent. Or David Leavitt. One of these people everybody says are geniuses. They all write like they're bored—they tell you what people are like by what's on their T-shirts. Like 'Save the Wetlands,' and you know it's an ecology type."

They rummage through their food—pappardelle with a wood-duck and porcini ragout, and seared salmon with wild-mushroom risotto. The restaurant around them broods in shadowy teal and fuchsia. Stray Greek columns support nothing but the idea of postmodern chic.

"The guy in the ad with Tama Janowitz," says the bond trader. "He's from back in the Kennedy administration—Arthur Schlesinger. What a great comeback shot for him."

"He writes books about history," she says. "There's a lot of nostalgia now. It's like everything's been on rerun since the sixties, people want to read about that stuff. They go crazy over anniversaries: Elvis's death, D day's fortieth, 1984 from that novel by George Orwell."

"You've got this literary side," he says. "You've definitely got this literary side."

"A lot of my clients want us to do the books along with the bookshelves. The classics: F. Scott Fitzgerald, Norman Mailer, anything leather-bound, morocco-bound. All the arts are like a religion now."

"Definitely," says the bond trader. "I know a commodities guy who's investing in painters. Julian Schnabel, he's so great—he gets to know all the right people in the art world, and then he figures out, nobody ever glued dishes to a painting before, and the next thing his prices are through the roof. My friend has five Schnabels. Never looks at them, just keeps them in storage."

"Basquiat did it without the dishes," the decorator says. "Then he went and OD'd. Do you know how great his stuff looks on walls? It's like, you don't have to pay any attention to it, but it's a great statement."

"I've got to get you to look at this place I bought in Brooklyn Heights. What time is it? We could get a cab. Talk about undecorated. Just me living there with the leather furniture I bought after my first bonus. Me and a small supply of Bolivian marching powder."

"I'd be happy to give you some advice, but I have to be up at six when my trainer arrives," she says, with a cool appraisal that concludes he's just another Wall Street trading-floor cowboy who feels obliged to go for a score; he doesn't really want it that much. She goes out with a lot of these types— she's been known to savor a score herself—and she thinks about men like a casting director, maybe because she thinks of her life as a movie. Last week there was this sad guy with a heavy upper lip and a motorcycle, the kind of guy who folds his hands behind his head and waits for you to come on to him, and you do—that's sex in the eighties.

The bond trader consoles himself . . . what the hell, even sex has become a sort of air-guitar duet. Both men and women fake orgasms now . . . too tired . . . work so hard,

too tired . . . cocaine . . . people talk about this new mood
elevator called Prozac. . . . He imagines Prozac producing
a sort of air-guitar happiness . . . maybe he'll ask his
shrink. . . .

1990–2000

Whatever

. . . we'd conquered reality . . .

E verything was so unpleasant at first. Even after we won a nifty Persian Gulf war over oil, President Bush said, "People are worried, there has been talk of decline."

The economy, the ecology, the homeless, a "nation at risk" . . . and then one day you realized the mood had lifted, and life now possessed a pleasant and prosperous vacancy, like a July suburb where the only sign of inhabitants was the exhaust from air conditioners shaking the hydrangeas.

Indifference was the preferred state of being, as if irony had become too much work. "Whatever" was the era's motto. Things drifted apart. Distance was desirable. Earlier postwar slang had celebrated hipness, the heightened awareness of reality. A new slang arose in the nineties to nullify reality.

"Brooke," you said. "If you're going swimming, your homework has to be done first."

"Whatever."

"You could end up grounded for the rest of the semester."

"As if," she said.

"As if what?"

"Don't go there, Dad."

"I just want to know the homework will be done," you said.

"Sure."

"Thank you."

"No problem."

Sometimes, being alive in the nineties could verge on the thrilling, like watching an acrobat stack impossible objects— a stool, a bicycle, a ball—and then stand on top with triumphant hands in the air. The acrobat was O. J. Simpson with his impossible acquittal after the dagger slaughter of his ex-wife; or Bill Clinton, who ultimately won forgiveness for his repeated bouts of oral sex with an intern in the White House (did puritan America envy his eerie absence of guilt and shame?); or the Dow Jones average, which quintupled for no reason anyone could explain except with words like *momentum,* which said only that it was rising because it was rising.

We hadn't lost our vitality as much as we'd conquered reality. We awakened one morning to find ourselves transformed by endless exoskeletons of technology: headphones, cell phones, Spandex, latex, Palm Pilots, laptops, Prozac, Internet porn, air bags, sneakers, Caller ID, Oakley sunglasses, whatever. We no longer had to rely on ordinary joys: the darkness of a June woods, the giddiness of a baby. Who had time for the idiot happenstance of reality? The age of epiphany was over. The age of downloading was here.

We triumphed over reality the way we once triumphed over wilderness, and we didn't know quite what to do next, except make money. It seemed as if existence itself had been franchised and outlets were everywhere: virtual-reality computer games, car CD players and faxes, MTV, Internet romance, theme parks, traffic jams, corporate cubicles, jail cells. (One out of 150 people in the Land of the Free was in prison or jail by the end of the nineties. What was wrong? What had they done? What had we done?)

White-collar women looked preoccupied and vexed, as if wondering whether they'd fed the cat that morning, or why their husbands were so boring. They moved through the world with an averted look, as if they were air-kissing reality itself. You watched them put on makeup while they drove to work, talked on cell phones, and honked the horns of cars that encapsulated them like pantyhose.

They lingered alone outside office buildings, smoked their exiled cigarettes, and looked oddly bitter, as if to imply that once, when life was more than work and money, they'd had mothers who taught that a lady never smokes on the street, especially when alone. They worried that sex made them happier than anything they did at the office, or it didn't make them happier than anything they did at the office. Martha Stewart made them worry that their homes weren't perfect. Television talk shows—Oprah Winfrey, Sally Jessy Raphael, Jenny Jones, Jerry Springer—consoled them with episodes like "Women Who Marry Their Rapists" or "When Daddy's Operation Turns Him into a Mommy."

Having been raised in the dark age of Freud, these women relaxed a little when they read that their children's happiness was now held to be controlled by genes, not toilet training. Breeding, in; upbringing, out. Nature over nurture. Meanwhile, tens of millions of Americans came to suspect misery was merely a matter of brain chemistry: that was the message of mood-elevating pills like Prozac and Zoloft.

"Manliness," as Teddy Roosevelt meant it, became a word that verged on the politically incorrect. The new male mandarins of medicine, law, media, and government didn't know how to do manhood anymore—even how to set their jaws or steady their gazes—but their power was so well buffered by bureaucracy that they didn't need the sort of face and walk that could command respect.

The older ones had been educated to prove our superiority over the Commies in the Cold War (as long as they didn't have to go to Vietnam), but now the Cold War was over and they seemed wistful in their triumph.

Occasional bombings of the archfiend of the moment — Saddam Hussein, Moammar Gadhafi, Osama bin Laden, Slobodan Milosevic—didn't have the same Armageddon profundity.

The younger ones sought careers where qualifications— SAT scores, titles—were more important than experience. The Doctrine of Experience had long since vanished, the Hemingwayesque notion that bright young men should go off and chip paint on tramp steamers or do some bar fighting in El Paso as part of their education and manliness. Taking risks now demonstrated foolishness instead of courage, and the younger men seemed to believe they could live forever if they ate skinned chicken and always wore a helmet while riding a bicycle.

Hemingway, of all people, was a hero to these guys. They bought Hemingway marlin-fishing hats and so on from the J. Peterman catalog (which went bankrupt), but it wasn't the young genius they admired, it was the crazy old graybeard celebrity—as if somehow, someday, they could cash in law partnerships, quit editorial boards, grow beards, and go off and be rich, admired, and true to themselves at last, the male equivalent of women's planning to have one perfect child in their forties.

Who could imagine being nostalgic for the nineties?

A yearning for the past is best provoked by smell, and by the nineties, we'd eradicated smells. People, animals, industries, seasons, love, and death smelled of nothing at all except deodorant: no burning leaves, sweat, bacon and eggs (eggs fried in the bacon grease of yesteryear until the edges got a little lacy), mothballs in summer attics, cigar smoke in fur coats, cabbage hallways in apartment houses, all of it whisked away by chemicals, environmental-protection laws, snobbery, range hoods, air conditioners, and washing as a nearly religious obsession. (Women's hair lost its thickness and mystery with daily scrubbing—it looked so dry you feared it would ignite from static electricity.)

Perhaps the world seemed to have lost its perfume because we'd grown older and lost our physical susceptibility to the ache of lilac or the possibilities in an old trunk. The median American was about thirty-six by the end of the century, compared with thirty in 1980 and twenty-three in 1900. In any case, smell was bad. It was too real. Some people sealed their windows and never smelled the iron dankness of November or the onion grass of spring; they just flipped the climate-control switch from "heat" to "cool." Weather was something we heard about on the radio, like a traffic jam.

Morality progressed, too. Hope became ambition, faith was optimism, charity was tolerance, honor was reputation, fame was celebrity, character was self-esteem, personality was life-style, absolutes were relative, unity was diversity, and destiny was whatever.

As always, we confused prosperity with possibility. After a bit of a recession, there were jobs for almost everyone, and the lower and middle classes came to believe with poignant certainty that they would never get poorer, while the rich could believe with condescending certainty that they would always get richer.

Those who liked to fear for our republic couldn't find much to fear. Campaign funding? Social Security? The globalization of American culture? The rise of Hillary Clinton as a Calvinist Eva Perón—a lady of perpetual personal sorrows, with a nobility that sprang from her refusal to do anything about them?

No bohemia or avant-garde worked at a usurpation of Establishment privilege: there was no Ralph Nader, no Timothy Leary or Jack Kerouac, no Abbie Hoffman leading mobs of demonstrators, no Allen Ginsberg warning, "America, I'm putting my queer shoulder to the wheel." To be famous for very long you had to be rich, a rule that kept most troublemakers out of the public arena. The closest thing to young rebels were characters in Doug Coupland's novel *Generation X:* "I seemed unable to achieve the animal happiness of people on TV. . . . I was on automatic pilot. . . . You really have to wonder why we even bother to get up in the morning. I mean really: why work? Simply to buy more stuff?"

No philosopher, scientist, revolutionary, foreign country,

or disease disturbed our equilibrium beyond the occasional static over schoolyard massacres or police maltreatment of African Americans. The gathering of black men in the Million Man March on the Mall comforted white America more than it threatened it.

Artists had been castrated years before by the corporate- and government-funded bureaucracies of museums and universities. No musician threatened to change the world in the manner of Elvis Presley; popular music had been conquered by dividing it into a thousand tastes. Music was under corporate control, though control started to leak out through the Internet with the downloading of whole compact discs for free. Rap artists stopped advocating the assassination of policemen. Outrage was impossible; vulgarities vanished into the tar baby of indifference. Nobody even whistled anymore.

Was there some kind of conspiracy here?

The most admired literary figure was the screenwriter, who surrendered all integrity and independence to producers, thereby practicing the aesthetics of indifference, of whatever.

Fashion became marketing, and slack-faced fashion models made nineties indifference visible with the look called heroin chic. In the age of credit cards, cash came to seem exotic until the Treasury produced new bills that looked as if they'd been printed in a country that spoke Esperanto. The new quarters had a Canadian lifelessness. For a whole century, cultural terrorists such as D. H. Lawrence and Norman Mailer had been firing torpedoes at repression, conformity, and power. By century's end, they had all proven themselves to be duds, though the lyrical dystopianism of William Burroughs held its appeal. Sex replaced sewing patterns as a how-to item in women's magazines: "How to Push His Hot Buttons and Make Him Beg You for More!" "The Non-Stop Orgasm—It's Real and You Can Have It!" It became a multi-billion-dollar industry of pornographic videos and Internet smut, and nobody cared much because nobody was scared of it anymore.

Sex wasn't really a nineties thing. The *New York Observer* wrote: "They love sex, but not as much as they love their Prozac. Forced to choose between designer drugs and prowess in the boudoir, the most fashionably medicated people go for the drug every time." The problem was that mood elevators could be libido deflators, and they were best-selling prescription drugs. Sensing a new market, pharmaceutical scientists came up with Viagra, a cure for impotence.

Whatever. In a 1998 Gallup Poll, 85 percent of Americans said they were satisfied with their personal lives—one of the highest percentages since Gallup began asking the question, in 1979—and 76 percent said they were satisfied with the future facing their families, one of the highest levels since 1963.

They worked harder than ever. "Multitasking" was a new work ethic: your boss flipped through memos, listened to somebody on the phone, and watched a computer monitor while he talked with you and his secretary. He seemed so distant. You felt so alone. Multitasking was the art of managing indifference, distance, and solitude.

A quarter of all households were occupied by just one person. In your office, you worked next to people you spoke to only by e-mail. Computer systems kept crashing to remind you that your life was controlled by distant, unpetitionable forces, not unlike the God of the eighteenth century, who retreated behind the clockwork of His universe and left man to his fate. Except the eighteenth-century God didn't crash. Computers did, ultimately teaching the virtue of indifference to those who had once raged at them.

Why bother? No one was responsible for these things; *things* were responsible for things. "The server is down." Or "We can't access the H drive." Whatever.

A new choice had been brought to America: elective loneliness. Memoirs replaced novels as the fashionable literary form. Golf replaced tennis as the fashionable sport. Internet games and chat rooms replaced social life, even offering the chance to change your identity and sign on as someone else.

We fled reality and ourselves. It was our right to do so. By the end of the century, it was a tradition, this fleeing that had begun with the great escape from a Victorian gloom of patriarchal fathers and Victorian brightness of theology; of the shame and guilt of thinking we're responsible for ourselves; and an escape, too, from the smell of woodsmoke and the ozone sparks of streetcars; from mothers preaching good posture, progress, and patriotism; from wool-clad crowds in seaside photographs, the glassy-eyed slums, the families with no choice but listening to Aunt Lil sing "'Tis the Last Rose of Summer" while a Sunday afternoon ticked away.

ILLUSTRATION CREDITS

ABOUT THE AUTHOR

Pulitzer Prize winner Henry Allen is a Marine veteran of Vietnam and a graduate of Hamilton College. Before joining the *Washington Post*, he covered the White House and Capitol Hill for the *New York News*, and backpacked through the late 1960s from New Mexico to Nepal. He is author of a novel, *Fool's Mercy*, a collection of essays, *Going Too Far Enough*, and a chapbook of poetry, *The Museum of Lost Air*. He has read his light verse with the National Symphony, taught an honors course in culture and meaning at the University of Maryland, and written for *The New Yorker*, *The New York Review of Books*, the *Paris Review* and *Vogue*. Father of three children, he lives with his wife in Takoma Park, Maryland.

This book was set in Fournier, a typeface named for Pierre Simon Fournier *fils* (1712–1768), a celebrated French type designer. Coming from a family of typefounders, Fournier was an extraordinarily prolific designer of typefaces and of typographic ornaments. He was also the author of the important *Manuel typographique* (1764–1766), in which he attempted to work out a system standardizing type measurement in points, a system that is still in use internationally. Fournier's type is considered transitional in that it drew its inspiration from the old style, yet was ingeniously innovational, providing for an elegant, legible appearance. In 1925 his type was revived by the Monotype Corporation of London.

Composed by North Market Street Graphics,
Lancaster, Pennsylvania

Printed and bound by RR Donnelley & Sons Company,
Harrisonburg, Virginia

Design by M. Kristen Bearse and Johanna S. Roebas